Captured by Grace

Intimately,
Intensely,
Intentionally

Jack Hager (with Milt Toratti)

LifeRich Publishing is a registered trademark of The Reader's Digest Association, Inc.

LifeRich Publishing books may be ordered through booksellers or by contacting:

LifeRich Publishing
1663 Liberty Drive
Bloomington, IN 47403
www.liferichpublishing.com
844-686-9607

Because of the dynamic nature of the Internet, any web addresses or links contained in this book may have changed since publication and may no longer be valid. The views expressed in this work are solely those of the author and do not necessarily reflect the views of the publisher, and the publisher hereby disclaims any responsibility for them.

Any people depicted in stock imagery provided by Getty Images are models, and such images are being used for illustrative purposes only.
Certain stock imagery © Getty Images.

ISBN: 978-1-4897-4057-1 (sc)
ISBN: 978-1-4897-4056-4 (hc)
ISBN: 978-1-4897-4062-5 (e)

Library of Congress Control Number: 2022903702

Print information available on the last page.

LifeRich Publishing rev. date: 03/16/2022

Contents

Preface vii

Introduction ix

Chapter 1   The Early Years with Family –Imprinted Values 1

Chapter 2   Search for Discipline and Leadership in
Military Service 11

Chapter 3   Witness to Leadership Failures............................. 17

Chapter 4   The Green Door Syndrome "'Attached' to
11th ACR... 27

Chapter 5   Potential Unfulfilled – Back in "The World"........ 39

Chapter 6   Downward Spiral to Rock Bottom........................ 43

Chapter 7   'SEE' to Jesus Christ as the only Authentic
Power (Being Tested) 53

Chapter 8   Life Changes with the Love of My Life................. 65

Tragedy of Suicide.. 83

Addendum-... 85

Preface

This "book" is, like its writer, weird.

The first couple pages will describe the birth of the book; all because of a "chance" meeting.

I will give a flyover view of my life.

My buddy Milt will share some insights and opinions.

My "dysfunctional" family, racism, booze, drugs, The "Pueblo", Vietnam, crime, prison, Christianity and more will be touched on.

Reading may entertain you, educate you, infuriate you, bless you, puzzle you.

If you give the time to read it, I am blessed and honored.

After (if?) you read, you may have questions, arguments, or just need a listening ear.

I'd love to hear from you:

Jack Hager
709 E Hyde Park Ave
Saint Joseph, MO 64504
jack.hager@gmail.com
816 261 1881

I blog at www.youcanknowjack.com and I chat on "You Know Jack – the Podcast"

Introduction

It was October 1st, 2021, and I was in my garage selling some of my military items. I noticed a fellow about my age pacing on the sidewalk while talking on his cell phone for quite some time. I saw how he proudly carried himself, his confident pace and he seemed to be very self-assured with whomever he was speaking with. He had a shirt on that read: "Graduate of University of South Vietnam-1968-1969". I said to myself: "this guy is a man of substance." I was also in Vietnam at the same time and then he came over to me after walking through my garage and looking at some of the military items for sale. He introduced himself as Jack Hager and shared that he had been attached to the 11th Armored Cavalry in Vietnam. Coincidentally, I had already written two Veteran oral histories for soldiers also serving in his unit (Dave Chappel and Jim McIntosh), so, we had something in common. Jack purchased a book on the History of the Vietnam War and the story: "We Were Soldiers, And Young" by LTC Harold G. Moore along with an autographed photo of Moore pictured with his CSM Basil Plumley. This interaction led us to talking about possibly writing Jack's Veteran oral history. Jack said to me: "Milt, I've had many people tell me that I need to write my story, and here we are discussing the same thing; I have a sordid tale to tell. I am a child of the 60's, I came from a broken and totally dysfunctional home, I was a bitter Vietnam Veteran voicing dissent against America after my experiences in combat, I'm an alcoholic, I'm a drug user, I'm a drug dealer, I am an ex-con, I was pretty much an overall scumbag…until Jesus invaded my life in a jail cell in Texas. I was arrested in Texas, spent a few months in jail there awaiting extradition; then an Oregon county sheriff picked me up and escorted me to Oregon, where I was later sentenced to a dime (ten years). While behind bars, the gospel captured me, and I trusted Jesus Christ. Since parole in 1977 I've served the Lord with Kansas City Youth for Christ, then Headwaters Christian Youth, (Rhinelander,Wisconsin), Family Life Ministries (Bath, New York), and since 2008 with Midland Ministries in Saint Joseph, Missouri. Additionally, I've served as a volunteer chaplain for various prison systems over four decades, and I've learned a few things and have insights, as well as being argumentative when needed." There was a pause to allow me to absorb his self-disclosure, and then Jack said: "Sir, are you up to dealing with such a complicated human such as I"? I said it would be an honor and privilege to hear his story, research, and collaborate with Jack to write his story.

Jack Hager was trained as an Army Security Agency specialist during the War in Vietnam with a top-secret clearance with duty in Korea, Germany and Vietnam. Jack was assigned to the 11th Armored Cavalry Regiment as an ASA specialist among the human intelligence (HUMINT), signal intelligence (SIGINT) 'Radio Research', interrogators and counter-intelligence specialists. The direct control of ASA units by the NSA became an irritant for Army field commanders during the Vietnam War because the ASA specialists were required to pass all information they gathered up the reporting chain to the NSA at Fort Meade, and were forbidden to share any classified intelligence with the units for whom they were attached. Such was the case for Specialist Jack Hager attached to the 11th Armored Cavalry Regiment. The NSA, which was primarily focused on strategic intelligence, often neglected valuable tactical intelligence, nor did they relay it to field commanders until too late for the intel to be of any tactical use. They were unknown because officially they did not exist. All were hidden at undercover designations to mask their true identities, with Radio Research Unit (RRU) being the most common designator. Frequently, the only intel firebase or garrison commanders got from ASA units was the inference that an attack might be underway when the local ASA-er, "Radio Research"-listening post began hurriedly tearing down its antennae and preparing for evacuation for disappearance from the battlefield. This ongoing intel failure became known as the "Green Door Syndrome". This changed after the war, when ASA units became organic to corps, division, and regimental headquarters; and ASA troops began being trained in the arcane (and pointless) art of "sanitizing" signal intelligence so as to conceal its origin and speed its delivery to supported commands. ASA enlisted personnel like Jack scored extremely high in the stringent mental requirements and many were more highly educated than the officers under whom they served; as well as having top secret clearances that the officers did not possess. Hence these specialists complied with the "Green Door Syndrome" and could not be challenged by the field commanders, regardless of commander's rank and stature.

ASA clandestine soldiers like Jack held copies of their orders and records in identical brown manila envelopes, and each soldier's medical records were stamped: If injured or killed in combat, report as training accident in the Philippines. The unit was so highly classified even its name was top-secret. It was given a codename, a cover identity to hide the true nature of its mission. The unit's operational headquarters was housed in a heavily guarded compound near Saigon. Its operatives such as Jack Hager were intercepting signal communications, then sending 'up the chain' for intelligence analysis and passing the information to the U.S. Military Assistance Advisory Group-Vietnam after sanitizing back in the U.S. Jack like other ASA service members were issued a special I.D. card which read:

The possessor of this document is on a classified military assignment. Do not detain or question him. He is authorized to wear civilian clothing, carry a weapon and pass into restricted areas.

While reading Chaplain Jack's story to include his time in prison cell #D-365 at the Oregon State Prison; you will find yourself humming the melody to Kris Kristofferson's song "Why Me Lord" which Kristofferson wrote in 1973. These two stanzas below are the true reflection of Jack's life over-and-over again, as Jack discovered his true passion and 'calling' in life. This is why I inserted these words as the sub-title to the book: "Try me, Lord, If you think there's a way, I can try to repay, All I've taken from you, Maybe Lord, I can show someone else, what I've been through myself, on my way back to you." Writing a Veteran oral history is really a personal biography and requires courageous disclosures. Jack's story like all the other biographies is very significant to preserve how history is shaped. I came to know Jack Hager as a man who stands up for the ideal of Faith and proactively seeks to improve the lives of others. So, Jack strikes out against injustice and counsels, preaches, teaches, advises, mentors and demonstrates to anyone at every opportunity his enthusiasm and energy as tiny ripples of Hope that builds momentum to sweep away walls. Knowing Jack Hager's mission statement is to know him best: I desire to know God intimately, so I can love God intensely; and to serve Him intentionally, while helping others do the same. (MT)

Reverend Hager's Commentary.

I call them "God-winks" – seemingly random events that, on closer investigation, are obvious divine appointments orchestrated by a loving and sovereign God.

It was the first day of October, 2021. My wife asked me to pick up a couple items in Saint Joseph. Enroute home I spotted a sign that pointed right and read, "Garage Sale." Why not?

As I turned, I noticed a much smaller poster that read, "Garage Sale – Military Items" and pointing down another street. Poof went the garage sale, and I pulled up to the house hosting the military sale. I got out and finished a phone call, and walked up the driveway in time to hear a gentleman say, "I've just finished my 99th book."

Say what? I asked him to explain, and he shared his passion for recording the history of veterans; particularly combat vets. I "qualified" and as we talked it seemed God was providing an answer to the urgings of many friends.

You see, I've got one of "those" testimonies. Fundamentally all Christ-followers have the same testimony – we once were lost, now we are found. But the details of my first 26 years of life were far different than most people. You'll read about some of that stuff in the pages to come.

Let me be frank…much of the story will be somewhat vague… not simply because I'm older-than-dirt and my memory may not be functioning correctly; not because of all the drugs/booze; but because there are things in my military years, criminal years, and trial proceedings that I simply cannot discuss. Not "won't," but "can't." (but, if you really want the details, call 1-800-urasucker and we'll get it to you. (sorry)

But because my story involves a lot of junk most people have not experienced, folks have been urging me to write a book for four decades. At first it was easy to say "no," because I knew back in those days in order to be published, I'd have to write a lot of detailed chapters about my "BC" days and maybe a chapter on my "AD" days.

Then came the dawn of self-publishing, and I thought/prayed about it. I never got clearance to invest the time to write. I was (and am) super busy, and it didn't seem good stewardship to carve out time to write. Just didn't seem like there would be enough juice for the squeeze.

Then came that October day, and now you get to read it. My prayer is that God is glorified, you are edified, and maybe even a bit entertained in reading this manuscript. Welcome to my world... it's been a rather weird ride, and I invite you to sort-of ride along...

Chapter 1

The Early Years with Family —Imprinted Values

Milt: Jack, Let's start with your family ancestry…what do you know about your family ancestry? Jack: Milt, it is important to understand the family dynamic regarding this first question. My mother and father were both what is termed 'socially acceptable alcoholics'. With this as the background, my mother especially constantly lied about everything; she fabricated what she perceived as the truth and I was told that my dad's dad (my grandfather) was in the German Navy and on a cruise to South America, I was told that he jumped ship somewhere along the Amazon River prior to World War I. He deserted the German Navy because he had distain for the Kaiser. Wherever he was in South America, he eventually worked his way to Gloucester, Mass., and there he was known as a 'model ship builder'; making large detailed wood models of clipper ships and hand-crafted ships inside large glass bottles.

I'm told that his ship models are on display in a Gloucester Museum and two family members did own a couple of those ship models, but I don't know where they are today. I don't know where my grandfather was born in Germany, nor do I know when and where he died. It would have been nice if I had met him and heard his story first-hand. I can only assume what they told me was truthful. So, I never met my grandparents on either side of the family. My mother said that her dad was a very wealthy Bostonian, and left it at that. I never met any other relatives other than one uncle, but don't know who's sibling he was.

A search on ancestry.com and myheritage.com revealed the following: John "Jack" Richard Hager was born to Harry J. Hager (1912-1996) and Esther F. [Barrett] Hager (1914-2009) in Cambridge, Massachusetts on June 1st, 1947. His older brother was Robert "Bob" Hager who followed his father into the Army military intelligence with counter-intelligence specialty. Jack's paternal grandparents were John Julius Hager (1880-1948) and Leona C. [Allman] Hager (1884-????). Grandfather John Julius Hager was listed as having immigrated to America in 1907 from Hamburg, Germany and naturalized in 1916, Boston, MA. Grandmother Leona was an American citizen born abroad in Estonia-Russia.

Jack's maternal grandparents were Clifton Addison Barrett (1889-1965) and Mary Ellen [O-Connor] Barrett (1891-1941) and both were from Brookline, MA. Maternal grandparents were Melvin Elbert Barrett (1868-1929) from Brattleboro, VT, and Mary Barrett (Stodder) from Boston, MA; and she received her education at Harvard. MT

Jack's father was a career Army NCO who rose to the rank of Master Sergeant with duty in the infantry and missile air defense. The family moved multiple times to include duty in Germany and his father was absent for extended times on permanent and temporary duty assignments.

Milt: Can you describe your childhood as best you can remember?
Jack: I was born on June 1st 1947, and according to my parents I had my tonsils taken out at 9 months old and they always said that I would have died had not my tonsils been removed. Really do not remember the very early years except for fleeting images when we lived in 'post-war Germany' at Stuttgart. My dad was assigned to the infantry; and we were not wealthy but had a maid named Elsie, which was quite normal in those days in Germany. I remember taking a train ride with Elsie along with our dogs "Lady" and "Toughie" which were a German Shepard and Dachshund. I was devastated when I was told at the age of five that our dogs could not return to America with us. My mother worked somewhere on post in a secretarial position to help support the family. My brother was in Frankfurt going to the DOD high school and his graduation party was in the Heidelberg Castle. We were a military family but I only remember living on post one time in Texas. I recall in Texas watching TV when we heard a tremendous explosion outside of El Paso. We later learned that it was a "flying wing" that crashed. It was an experimental aircraft that looked like a single wing.

My next memory is Massachusetts. We lived in a very small apartment where I could touch both walls from my bed. My mother occasionally sent me down to the local bakery to purchase fresh baked French bread. I'd always get chewed out because and on the way home, I'd bite off the ends of the loaf of bread.

The move I remember the most was to Newhall, California and there was a small military housing area surrounded by a cyclone fence in the middle of nowhere with the missile site on top of 'magic mountain'. Now that area is all built up with $500,000 homes. Sand Canyon was military housing, and my dad was no longer in the infantry but converted to missile defense across the country with the Nike Ajax and Hercules missile sites. We were stationed in a location so he could cover about 5 missile sites to include the underground site on 'magic mountain'. We lived over the hill in Sand Canyon with about 40 homes. Across the street was a black guy married to a German girl. They had two kids; one was dark black, the other looked white. This was in the early sixties. Everyone got along. The high school I went to in Southern California was mostly white, but had a good percentage of blacks and what we then called "Chicanos," Mexican Americans. I had friends in all ethnic and racial identities.

My theft habit started early when I was about 11 or 12 years old when I was at a hardware store with my dad. There was a display of fishing lures and I snatched two or three of the lures and put them in my pocket. As we departed the store, a security guy caught up with us and I could not get rid of the lures quick enough because the hooks had impaled me. It was not the brightest thing I ever did.

My dad took me back inside to apologize to the store owner and tried to teach me a lesson. Then when I was 13 years old, I had a close buddy Julio Garcia and obviously we could not buy cigarettes or alcohol. But Julio's dad who could not speak a word of English would buy us the alcohol.

I attended high school at William S. Hart High School in Newhall, California and I was not academically challenged, but mostly bored. I was in the top 10% of the class and I did not often attend classes in my junior and senior years. I had started drinking a lot by the age of 12 or 13 and was a very serious drinker. I self-diagnosed myself as an alcoholic by the time I was a junior in high school. I was a great talker, a 'con-man' who could manipulate and bamboozle anyone. No one in high school knew that I was a thief who robbed liquor stores and would steal anything. I was fairly popular, and my best subject was journalism with Edwin "Ed" Murdock as the teacher/advisor who desperately cared for his students. Mr. Murdock took me under his wing and in my freshman year I was a writer, sophomore year a reporter, and then the sports editor with the capstone as the editor in chief of the "Smoke Signals" Hart High School Indians newspaper in my senior year.

My dad received orders for Korea on an unaccompanied tour, so mom and I lived in a small apartment until he returned about 12 or 18 months later. Upon return, he was reassigned to Northern California and I did not want to go with them on this move. So, they told me, if I could find a family to stay with, I could finish school on my own. Essentially, we were mutually estranged from that point on. I did find a buddy whose family took me in their home, and my parents came to my graduation the following year. That was the last time I saw my dad. He died in a VA hospital sometime in the 1990's, and you found the exact date in your ancestry search. I saw my mother one time after that when I flew from New York back to California to visit my brother Bob and his family.

In the mid-nineties I got a call from my sister-in-law informing me that my father was in critical condition and not expected to live long. He was hospitalized in a Veterans Administration facility near Richmond, California.

After thinking/praying/discussing with my wife, I wrote a letter to him asking permission to come see him. I sent it certified mail to ensure that he received it, as I was pretty certain my mother would destroy it rather than give it to him.

I later learned that my brother was in the room when the letter was delivered and signed for. Bob told me my Dad told Mom to contact me and invite me to visit.

I never received any communication from my mother.

My father died from prostate cancer in 1996.

Besides the Vietnam War, there were two other vivid national news events that drew focus in those years. The assassination of President John F. Kennedy on Nov. 22nd, 1963, was very traumatic. I was in class when a student named Lloyd Allen Foote came running into class and said: "The President was shot, The President was shot". Because I thought it was a joke, I said "What's the punchline?" I wasn't devastated by the assassination as most people were; but more intrigued with the circumstances and trying to figure out the motivation of the assassin. That night we cruised up and down Hollywood boulevard drinking beer and watching the reaction of the people on the street.

I played football and found it too much work; plus, the coach said that if he caught me drinking or smoking that I'd be off the team. Originally, I thought he was bluffing, but he wasn't, and he caught me drinking and I was off the team. I wrestled and active in the newspaper in a clique of six guys with similar interests.

Shortly after I graduated in 1965 the "Watts Riots" took place. Watts is in the inner city of Los Angeles and witnessed the first major race riot that occurred with I was in basic training at Fort Ord. Our basic training unit was alerted to potentially be involved with riot control duty as a result of the rioting to protect the streets.

[The Watts Rebellion, also known as the Watts Riots, was a large series of riots that broke out August 11, 1965, in the predominantly Black neighborhood of Watts in Los Angeles. The Watts Rebellion lasted for six days, resulting in 34 deaths, 1,032 injuries and 4,000 arrests, involving 34,000 people and ending in the destruction of 1,000 buildings, totaling $40 million in damages.] (MT)

MILT: Was your father, a Master Sergeant, the male influence in your life?

Jack: (after a pause)… I don't ever remember being disciplined by my father. We didn't do much as a family. He'd come home from work and sit in his easy chair and fix two martini drinks. He'd drink one and mother drank the other martini after she'd been drinking all day long. Then they'd drink beer and dad would pass out, mom would go upstairs to bed. I essentially took care of myself. My brother Bob was more of a mentor and father-figure than my dad. He taught me now to drive our Rambler Metropolitan car with a stick shift. I remember driving on Interstate-5 in a rainstorm and I thought we were going to float away in that tiny car. My brother Bob was eleven years older than me and enlisted in the Army right out of high school. He was stationed in Presidio of California in the CIC (Counter-Intelligence Corps) with military intelligence. He contracted diabetes and received a medical discharge. It was a waste for the Army to release such a dedicated intelligence asset, especially after investing so much time and money training Bob. He was highly proficient in his job, and he was very hurt by this terrible bureaucratic decision.

Milt: How did you get the money to fund your drinking and smoking? Jack: I did smoke cigarettes at an early age. I was a 'stringer' working for a local paper where I wrote articles on sports and made some money. But I got money by stealing. The first thing I remember stealing was $80 from my brother. Bob was home on military leave and got drunk. He was sleeping on the couch and his wallet was available. I saw about $300 in his wallet and took $80, hoping he wouldn't miss it. That led me to steal from kids in school, stealing from cars, stealing anything where the opportunity presented itself. At age 14 or 15, I obtained a pistol and went into LA to rob liquor stores. My drug of choice was Coors-Jack Daniels and Johnny Walker Red.

My only real arrest occurred as a junior in high school. I was working on the front-page of the school paper and the idea was to photograph the cheerleaders amongst a large group of pumpkins. Mr. Murdock gave us some money and told us to go buy some pumpkins. The area was very rural and after loading the pickup truck with pumpkins and ready to leave, we noticed a huge stack of crates loaded with pumpkins. Like wise guys we tipped over the crates of pumpkins that workers had slaved over to fill. We tipped over crate after crate for no reason other than malicious mischief. We were driving back to the school with the pumpkin load when a honking pickup truck pulled up alongside and a Mexican guy held up a sign with our license plate number written on it. We followed these Hispanics to the local LA County Sheriff's office and that was my first introduction to jail.

We remained over night in jail and later ordered to appear in front of the judge who yelled admonishments against us for our stupidity. The judge forced us to make restitution by going out on Saturday to work at that same farm. We husked corn, and drank tequila with the Mexican field workers as our punishment for six hours of restitution.

Milt: What kind of pistol was it? Did you have ammo and ever use it?

Jack: It was a .38 caliber pistol that I never fired. I never even practiced with it. I kind of wandered purposefully in the wrong side of L.A. and was approached by a black guy from whom I bought the pistol. I may have paid about fifty bucks for it. I then stuck it in people's faces which was more convincing than just demanding that they give me their money. I'm trying to think what I did with the pistol, but it seems that I probably threw it off the Malibu Pier into the ocean before I entered the Army.

Milt: It seems that Ed Murdock may have been a role model for you.

Jack: Edwin "Ed" Murdock and English teacher Lucie Rea impacted my life, and continue to do so, more than any other educator (until I got to Bible school!). I had Ed for three years, primarily for Journalism classes. Ed was a young teacher, friendly, caring, making the time to teach not class, but students. He later moved into counseling and administration... He was fun. Back then beer cans had 'pop tops', but there was not a "protector" around the tab, so every Monday, Mr. Murdock would check a few of us for "pop top thumbs." Opening the cans frequently resulted in deep scratches on the thumb.

He was a good man. I did not know he was a Christian then... then again, I didn't know what a Christian was. I honestly don't remember him ever mentioning Christ or faith...but I am sure he would pray for me...and so many others. After graduation we lost touch, but then in around 1980 I bumped into him while I was doing an assembly at Hart. He began supporting me financially at that point, and, at his homegoing, was my longest-standing financial supporter. He was a prayer warrior also...his significant financial giving will be replaced; his prayers not. My family was able to meet him several years ago, and a few years ago I got to pay him a visit with classmate Bob Satterfield. I miss his phone calls. I miss him.

There are 'power groups' in society that include the (1) police and courts, (2) government, (3) parents, (4) peer pressures, (5) teachers and schools, (6) clergy and church. Jack was exposed to the influential powers of peer pressure, parents, teachers, government and police by the age of eleven which 'imprinted' his values that guided him for the next seven years through high school graduation. However, the 6th power group of clergy and church were absent. After graduation the next five years began with Jack's search for discipline and meaningful leadership in the Army and a potential career in the military that followed his brother's example. Jack observed that 1965 was the pivotal year for America. Divorce became fashionable, mothers started to work away from home, latchkey kids became a norm, American flags were burned, hippies were promoted as cool, respect for authority began to slip, and marijuana replaced the beer can and booze, and schools were prohibited from providing religious instruction. (MT)

Chapter 2

Search for Discipline and Leadership in Military Service

After high school I received a scholarship to UCLA, but did not want to go to college. Vietnam was by that time in full swing and anti-war protests were everywhere and on TV constantly. The draft meant surefire duty in Vietnam, so I first visited the Navy recruiter but it did not work out. The Army recruiter had me take some aptitude tests which I passed with flying colors and the recruiter said I scored in the top 10% of the ASVAB: Armed Services Vocational Aptitude Battery tests. He declared that because of that high score I qualified for the Army Security Agency (ASA) and told me if I enlisted for four years, I'd stay in the U.S. and never see Vietnam. I went to Fort Ord, California for basic training for 8 weeks in 1965. It was a tough experience, but I was in good enough condition to take the abuse. We slept head-to-foot to keep us separated in the barracks due to infectious diseases like meningitis that were prevalent at that time. I never left base, and my drill instructor was a very senior NCO who had been in the Army, then to the USMC, and back into the Army. He was very typical for his discipline training and leadership.

After basic training I flew to Fort Devens, Ma for advanced training. I landed at Logan Airfield in Boston where the military shuttled me to the base. Fort Devens was the primary training site for Army Security Agency. I remember the "ditty-boppers" who were Morse Code Interceptors. The 'ditty-bopper's' training rooms had bars on the windows to control their raucous antics because they were so crazy and loony. The bars were added after a frazzled trainee tossed a massive military typewriter through the window.

ASA MOS codes:

05B-Linguist (Not used after the Vietnam War)
05D-Radio Direction Finding operators (a/k/a "Duffies")
05G-Communications & signal security specialists (a/k/a "Buddy fu_ _ _ _ _")
O5H-Morse code interceptors ("Ditty-boppers" or "Hogs")
05K-Non-Morse/non-voice (teletype & fax) intercept operators
98B-Cryptanalysis technician
98C-Signal intelligence analysts
98G-Voice intercept operators
98J-Non-communications (radar/telemetry) intercept & analysis techs
98K-Signal collection/ID analyst (4)

O5G30 communications security analyst was my MOS...and when debriefed we signed a non-disclosure agreement that stated we could not talk to anyone about what we did for the rest of our life. If we were caught revealing our mission and duties, we were told we'd spend the rest of our life in Leavenworth Prison. Like most things, bureaucrats probably over-classified our missions, but those were the rules and remain so yet today.

In our AIT training I continued drinking whenever I could. We were taken out for 'Jungle Warfare-Escape and Evasion' training at Fort Devens in the winter. Remember, Vietnam winters were known for torrential monsoons….not snow. This E&E program was developed by Colonel Millette. Col. Millette earned the Medal of Honor for leading the last bayonet charge in Korea. He was amazing; he wore a handle-bar mustache and stayed in the field with us. Col. Millett did not ask us to do anything that he did not do himself. He was the definition of a 'leader by example'. We conducted ambushes, counter-ambushes and we went through the protocol of escape, then capture, followed by interrogation and escape. They took us into a mock-Vietnamese village with the cadre who were mostly Korean Americans to add to the realism. They badgered us into spitting on the American flag, urinating on the American flag and denying allegiance to America. They connected wires from a crank phone to our skin that caused electrical current to flow through our bodies which was painful. At the end of the torture, we were placed in a hut…to discover a hidden tunnel that we crawled through, exiting quite a distance from the village. From there we had to make our way to the "friendly farmer" a couple miles away.

[CITATION: Capt. Millett, Company E, distinguished himself by conspicuous gallantry and intrepidity above and beyond the call of duty in action. While personally leading his company in an attack against a strongly held position he noted that the 1st Platoon was pinned down by small-arms, automatic, and antitank fire. Capt. Millett ordered the 3d Platoon forward, placed himself at the head of the 2 platoons, and, with fixed bayonet, led the assault up the fire swept hill. In the fierce charge Capt. Millett bayoneted 2 enemy soldiers and boldly continued on, throwing grenades, clubbing and bayoneting the enemy, while urging his men forward by shouting encouragement. Despite vicious opposing fire, the whirlwind hand-to-hand assault carried to the crest of the hill. His dauntless leadership and personal courage so inspired his men that they stormed into the hostile position and used their bayonets with such lethal effect that the enemy fled in wild disorder. During this fierce onslaught Capt. Millett was wounded by grenade fragments but refused evacuation until the objective was taken and firmly secured. The superb leadership, conspicuous courage, and consummate devotion to duty demonstrated by Capt. Millett were directly responsible for the successful accomplishment of a hazardous mission and reflect the highest credit on himself and the heroic traditions of the military service.] (1)

Milt: Here's my issue with your ASA training. You received a Top-Secret clearance which means that the FBI did a deep dive into your background as an 18-year-old who was estranged from his parents, had an incident with the police in the 'great pumpkin caper' and other incidents. Do you know if the FBI did the normal background investigation? Jack: I only learned of the investigation after arriving in South Korea. In school most of us had "provisional" security clearances, pending such an investigation. I arrived in Korea to find out my clearance still wasn't finalized...thus I could not do my job.

I stayed at base camp doing little until they assigned me to drive a colonel around the country. That only lasted a couple weeks...when I was replaced by a South Korean officer.

After maybe three months in-country I was ordered to report to the intelligence officer. Upon arriving I was read my rights by a Criminal Investigation Department agent. He asked, "Why did you not report on your enlistment application that you had been arrested on two occasions, to include once for armed robbery?" I honestly replied, "Because my recruiter said not to since I had no convictions."

The investigator believed me, and in a week or so my clearance became official, probably because I hadn't got into any trouble so far in my Army career, and they didn't want to invest the money and time put into my training. Some buddies back home later told me they were interviewed by CID and/or FBI agents during that time frame.

Milt: The ASA trained specialists were in SIGINT and HUMINT as well as interrogation and counter-intelligence. Which specialty were you? Jack: We were labeled 'buddy f_ _ _ _ _ _' because we monitored friendly communications and snooped to find out what was being communicated via telecommunications, teletypes, radio telephones and landlines. And we lived up to our identity.

Chapter 3

Witness to Leadership Failures

ASA Korea and Germany-

Milt: You were assigned to Korea, what was the unit designation?

Jack: I was assigned to Detachment A, 508th ASA Group, Uijeongbu, Korea. Korea was my favorite assignment. I first remember the stench when getting off the plane. As I disembarked from the plane an old 'papa-son' came running up to me with an extended handshake, and said: "Thank you for coming to my country". South Korea was the only duty station where I felt appreciated for serving. There were 10 of us who replaced the former battalion which was sent to Vietnam. We performed the communications security mission and we were all very young. No one messed with us because the perceived unknown fear of the ASA due to our secrecy. Heck, we didn't know what we were doing, why should anyone else?

Our shoulder patch was pretty impressive – a lightning bolt held by an eagle's claw. Sometimes we told gullible people that ASA stood for "Airborne Shock Assault." Not everyone realized we were kidding.

Korea was a 12-month tour. I liked the duty and the country so much that I put in for a year extension that was soon granted. I made E-5 quickly as stripes were overabundant because of the slots vacated by men killed in Vietnam.

About a year before I left Korea, General Charles Bonesteel took command of the 8th Army and U.N. forces.

Let me preface this story by describing our living situation. Again, we replaced a battalion, so many of the buildings were vacant. The ten of us were housed in a barracks that had maybe a dozen individual rooms. For military housing, it was spectacular. We had house girls who took care of everything, and a super-tall Korean/Black who served as our mechanic.

Next to the housing was our operations area. It consisted of an entry room, and then security doors leading to the actual operation area. Two of us had to be in the entry room 24/7 to ensure no unauthorized personnel tried to get in the ops area.

One afternoon I was on guard duty. The door opened and in walked a full-bird Colonel and General Bonesteel. My buddy and I leapt to our feet, stood at attention, and saluted.

The Colonel said something like, "This is General Bonesteel, and he is assuming command. We will now inspect your facility."

I took a breath and said, "Sir, with all due respect, you may inspect this room, as well as the barracks next door and our motor pool; but you cannot enter the operations area."

The Colonel went postal, screaming at us about rank and privilege and so forth.

He finally ran out of breath and questioned, "Exactly what are you going to do if we try to open that door?"

I happily replied, "Sir, if you or the general attempt entry I will have to shoot you."

He was not pleased. Bonesteel didn't say a word. They left.

A week or so later I received a Letter of Commendation from the General for doing my job and not caving in. I don't think the Colonel was pleased.

[Charles Hartwell Bonesteel III, was a 1931 graduate of the United States Military Academy at West Point, Bonesteel received from his classmates the lifelong nickname of "Tick." After graduation, he was a Rhodes Scholar at the University of Oxford. Bonesteel served as the Commander of U.S. Forces Korea (and Commander-in-Chief, U.N. Command Korea; Commanding General, Eighth U.S. Army) from 1966 to 1969. During this period he defended against North Korean infiltration during the Korean DMZ Conflict (1966-1969) and dealt with tensions arising from the January 1968 Pueblo Incident.]

JACK CONTINUES: While still in Korea an incident occurred that is an inkling of my "job". The Redeye was a highly classified, shoulder-fired surface-to-air missile system, and we were given specific orders to listen to any conversation regarding Redeye, to include the use of the word Redeye. It was a security violation to even utter or type the word "Redeye." I was monitoring phones when I heard two Lieutenants talking on the phone about when they were picking up some Redeyes on a specific time and date. So, I alerted my supervisor and turned over the recording. He took it….and the feedback story was that they were arrested, sent back to the States and served time in Leavenworth just for using the term Redeye.

Lots of stuff happened in Korea that was not well known in the states. The North sent an assassination team to kill President Pak. It was not successful, but our base was fired on with small arms during that tension. The North Korean invaders, dressed in South Korean uniforms, were captured within miles of the Presidential palace and subsequently executed.

We heard rumors of American Special Forces jumping into heavily wooded areas in the middle of South Korea to search for infiltrators. The rumors said the troops were never heard from again.

But the low light of my tour in Korea was the capture of the spy ship "Pueblo." Most Americans today have no clue what that refers to. It happened just after the assassination attempt.

On the 23rd of January, 1968 an Army major flew into our area, pulled us all into the operations area, and briefed us…The US ship Pueblo had been attacked and seized by the North Koreans. It apparently was going to be sailed into a North Korean harbor along with its 93 crewmembers." (We later learned that one was killed in the attack.)

I immediately was scared. In fact, I have never…not in Vietnam, not in prison, not anywhere…been as frightened. Why? Because (of my security clearance and need-to-know) I was aware that everything we had in South Korea was nuclear. I really thought that we were going to go to nuclear war, because (silly me) I had no clue the government would sell those guys out.

We went to highest alert status, but nothing happened. By the time some jets with conventional weapons arrived from Japan the Pueblo had entered Wonsan harbor. Later I learned the crew were paraded in front of national media, and then shipped to a series of secret detainment facilities. Torture and beatings were routine. Occasionally propaganda photos were taken of the men playing sports...all of whom had their middle finger extended to indicate they were forced to pose.

The surviving crew members were finally released on December 28, 1968.

The Pueblo a Banner-class environmental research ship, attached to Navy intelligence as a spy ship, in international waters, which was attacked and captured by North Korean forces on 23 January 1968, in what was later known as the "Pueblo incident" or alternatively, as the "Pueblo Crisis". The seizure of the U.S. Navy ship and her 83 crew members, one of whom was killed in the attack, came less than a week after President Lyndon B. Johnson's State of the Union address to the United States Congress, a week before the start of the Tet Offensive in South Vietnam during the Vietnam War and three days after 31 men of North Korea's KPA Unit 124 had crossed the Korean Demilitarized Zone (DMZ) and killed 26 South Koreans in an attempt to attack the South Korean Blue House (executive mansion) in the capital Seoul. The taking of Pueblo and the abuse and torture of her crew during the subsequent eleven months became a major Cold War incident, raising tensions between western and eastern powers. Pueblo was taken into port at Wonsan and the crew was moved twice to prisoner-of-war (POW) camps. The crew members reported upon release that they were starved and regularly tortured while in North Korean custody. This treatment turned worse when the North Koreans realized that crewmen were secretly giving them "the finger" in staged propaganda photos. Commander Lloyd M. Bucher was psychologically tortured, including being put through a mock firing squad in an effort to make him confess. Eventually the North Koreans threatened to execute his men in front of him, and Bucher relented and agreed to "confess to his and the crew's transgression." Bucher wrote the confession since a "confession" by definition needed to be written by the confessor himself. They verified the meaning of what he wrote, but failed to catch the pun when he said "We paean the DPRK [North Korea]. We paean their great leader Kim Il Sung". (Bucher pronounced "paean" as "pee on.]

As my second tour wound down, I wanted to extend again and be discharged right in Korea. My plan was to hook up with a Korean girl, open a bar, and stay there the rest of my days.

That request was turned down, so I submitted my "Dream Sheet," a formal request for duty stations. We were allowed to request three locations – I put in for Thule, Greenland; Synop, Turkey, and another "hardship" tour I can't remember. Why? I still did not want to go to Vietnam. The military, with its never-ending wisdom, instead sent me to Germany, which is typically a three-year tour.

Arriving in Germany, I reported to the Commanding Officer. This was early 1968. The timeframe is important. The CO was an African-American who had worked his way from enlisted to officer status.

I entered his office, saluted, and said "Specialist Hager reporting, Sir." He had my file in his hands. After a few moments he looked up and observed, "You are an E-5, correct?"

"Yes, sir."

He looked (glared?) at me and said, "You are on your first enlistment. You've only been in the Army about three years. You don't deserve your stripes and I am going to do all I can to take them away from you."

Was it a racist act? I think so. Regardless, I was pretty sure this guy was not going to be my favorite officer, and I was certain this was going to be a rotten duty assignment.

A couple weeks later we were again, as in Korea, called into a secure building and given another briefing. Radio traffic and other intel indicated the Russians were about to invade Czechoslovakia. We were ordered to prepare to move from our duty station (Herzo Base; a former German Air Force installation that still had trees growing on the roofs to elude allied bombers) to various stations along the Czech border so we could monitor (not prevent) the invasion and gather combat intelligence, both physical and electronic.

So, we covered up the nomenclature (identification) on our vehicles and moved out. My unit traveled to Hof Air Force Base where we were to spend the evening before moving on.

Little did I know I'd come under fire for the first time while on this base. Early that evening we were returning from the mess hall. A group of black airmen were walking to the mess hall...and they walked right by us.

Our lieutenant, who was from some Southern state, yelled at them. "Hey, boys, don't you salute an officer?" I was not thrilled that he used the word 'boys'. Remember…this is 1968. The airmen were not thrilled either, but they gave a reluctant salute and moved on.

Shortly after midnight a large group of black troops basically attacked us in our temporary barracks. Apparently, they did not realize we were authorized to carry M16s while they had M14s. We laid down suppressing fire and they exited. To the best of my knowledge no one was hit, but we quickly saddled up and moved out to watch the Russians do their invasion thing.

[Approximately 500,000 Warsaw Pact troops attacked Czechoslovakia, with Romania and Albania refusing to participate. East German forces, except for a small number of specialists, did not participate in the invasion because they were ordered from Moscow not to cross the Czechoslovak border just hours before the invasion. 137 Czechoslovakian civilians were killed and 500 seriously wounded during the occupation. The invasion successfully stopped Alexander Dubček's Prague Spring liberalization reforms and strengthened the authority of the authoritarian wing within the Communist Party of Czechoslovakia (KSČ). The foreign policy of the Soviet Union during this era was known as the Brezhnev Doctrine.] (MT)

Herzogenaurach Field Station was home to the 318th ASA Battalion. Their specialty was intercepting and analyzing radio and telephone traffic, as well as cryptology; over and above this, ASA was responsible for army communication security. When the electronic intelligence units of the U.S. Army in Europe were reorganized, the battalion was moved to Augsburg in 1971.

Milt: How old were you then? Jack: I was 21. While in the field for the Czech fiasco I 1049ed (volunteered) for Vietnam. Not because I wanted to go, but because there were only two ways out of Germany. Re-enlist or go to the Nam. As we said, I wouldn't re-enlist for two days for a three-day pass, so I volunteered to go to Southeast Asia.

Chapter 4

The Green Door Syndrome
"Attached' to 11th ACR

Jack: In Korea it was the 508th ASA Group, in Germany the 507th ASA Group, and because the ASA was not supposed to be in Vietnam; the ASA renamed us the 509th Radio Research Group and we wore different unit patches as a cover instead of ASA patches on our uniforms. Rumors were that the NVA had bounties on any member of the ASA; but these rumors were never fully substantiated.

The Radio Research Unit at Tan Son Nhut Air Base on the edge of Saigon, occupied a small white stucco headquarters near the flight line.

Milt: Your locations were identified by the NVA according to your antennae. The 11th Armored Cavalry command and staff also had the antennae and these were prime targets by the NVA. When too many of the commander's ACAV's were lost, then dummy antennae were randomly placed on other troop ACAV's to reduce the risk of losing leaders in the field.

Milt: On what airline did you fly into Bien Hoa?

Jack: I think I flew on TWA to Vietnam and my first impression of Vietnam was about the same as landing in Korea; but the stench was not as pungent. The Radio Research guys were separated from the larger group of soldiers, and I was "attached" to the 11th ACR while others were sent to Special Forces units. We were assigned to three ACAV's (Armored Cavalry Assault Vehicles) and specially outfitted for our equipment.

I was attached to the 11th Armored Cavalry Regiment, but not to any specific 'troop'. We had a crew of six ASA personnel in our ACAV and tagged along behind units into the field. We lived with the grunts in the field the entire tour of duty. I carried an M-16 rifle and fired the .50 caliber and M-60 machine guns. I was not qualified on these automatic weapons but learned to fire them quickly in that OJT combat environment. We also carried the M-79 grenade launcher for protection. The reason for 6 crew members was because of 24-7 monitoring of security communications. We'd have regular shifts and at times I traded shifts to get away from the heat and humidity outside. It was exceedingly tight inside the ACAV because of the commo equipment. Even the assigned driver was an ASA soldier and learned to drive the track OJT.

Milt: On paper you were likely assigned to Headquarters Company for the Regiment, but not tied to the chain of command. Jack: That's likely the assignment, but we did not report to the tactical chain of command. Our reports went up the ASA channels of communications and we never knew the results of our records, reports or recordings. We never knew if our battlefield intel ever completed the circular route back to the field commanders in the command vehicles next to us. We never received feedback because our operations were so secretive, and the need to know was above my pay grade. We did not exist as far as the Army was concerned.

But while some of our guys were monitoring enemy commo, I continued to listen in on American communications. Some of the stuff was pretty wild, but now and then we'd hear a unit accidentally give their position in the clear rather than in code; and we'd immediately run to the command track to advise the Cav guys of the compromise. They'd immediately get in contact with the unit that had been compromised and move them out to another location. I like to think just that intel action saved lives.

The South Vietnamese Army, Vietnamese linguists and interpreters as well as Korean ROK troops were in the field with us as well, but we did not interact with any of them. We just tagged along like a shunned stepchild, made our reports and no one messed with us. The troopers just looked at us for our oddity and disrespected us as less worthy of their combat assignments and weapons proficiency. I was the supervisor (track commander) of my ACAV and we only mingled with the cavalry troopers at mealtimes or picking up some supplies. In Vietnam I was on a constant "buzz" with marijuana and alcohol. A couple times I skin-popped heroin, but I was pretty scared of that drug.

Contrary to most of the Nam movies, not all Americans used drugs; I'd say it was a large chunk, but not the majority. Again, this is 19687-69, drugs were relatively new to the States and most of us had not imbibed until our military time.

My ACAV (Armored Cavalry Assault Vehicle) was not the only military vehicle named "Proud Mary" in Vietnam; but as we rode with the 11th Armored Cavalry, we'd often have the song blasting as much as a cassette player could blast!

Milt: I heard that soldiers in the ACAVS slept on the ammo cans and used their flak jackets for pillows...was that your case as well?
Jack: We just slept on the steel floor and never saw a bunk. It was a spartan existence in the field.

Milt: Your ACAV had an antennae, and also the Troop Commander's ACAV had an antenna because of special communications equipment aboard.

Jack: We had a normal ACAV but special racks were mounted inside for radio and intercept technology. We carried the normal ammo cans loaded with .50 cal., 7.62mm ammo belts, 5.56mm rounds and the M79 grenades and shotgun rounds. There were times when we fired our machine guns in convoy security, but nothing like the troopers constantly on dismounted patrols or assault missions. Once we received an RPG (rocket propelled grenade) that exploded next to our track in May, 1969. We were attacked by the NVA 274th Regiment and I was on the '50' when the rocket exploded near our track and knocked me to the ground. I was disoriented, dazed, but not wounded. None of the other crew members were wounded; but we probably all had various degrees of concussions. The shrapnel luckily did not hit any of us.

As I lay on the ground the firefight continued...I couldn't move. But two guys...who happened to be black...zoomed out to me and dragged me behind another track. They moved out and I was never able to thank them.

Milt: Col. George S. Patton was your regimental commander. Did you ever cross his path or what can you tell me about him?

Jack: I crossed paths with Patton once. I was inside my track alone and smoking marijuana. The rear entry opened and there was Colonel Patton staring me in the eye. He said: "Is that marijuana I smell, Hager?" I had no choice but to say, "Yes, Sir," to which he replied, "If I ever catch you smoking weed again, I'll shoot you." There was no doubt in my mind that he would follow through if given the opportunity. He was much like Col. Millette, a soldier's soldier, and was in the field with the troops to know what was going on.

The movie "Apocalypse Now" is ridiculous as far as accurately portraying Nam, but whoever wrote the script had to know of Colonel Patton...the actor Robert Duvall is Patton; hanging out of the command helicopter shooting his .45 at the enemy.

Milt: Your ASA crew of six with a 'top secret' mission and executing the 'greendoor policies' of bureaucracy, appears to have had almost total anonymity in the field. Were there ever any senior NCO's, officers, plain-clothed civilians who would inspect your field operations?

Jack: Nope. There just weren't many Agency guys around, to include officers. Again, even though we were called "Radio Research" anyone with an IQ three points higher than an aardvark would know we were Agency...and they were scared of us because they didn't know who we were or what we did. All some of them knew is that our chain of command bypassed the normal channels. Our higher up was the National Security Agency.

In an effort to further validate the 'greendoor syndrome', I discovered that most U.S. fighter pilots had no idea of the NSA's frequent intercept of NVA communications to include information about MiG flights. Some intelligence analysts intercepted North Vietnamese transmissions and classified the communications so the American pilots who did not have proper security clearances were kept out of the loop. Thus, this policy undoubtedly would have aided American pilots; but the intelligence wizards stated that using the information too frequently risked alerting the NVA that the U.S. was intercepting their signals.

Thus, they kept jeopardizing the pilots lives due to bureaucratic policy. The dilemma for American planners back in the United States was to decide upon a balanced use of the data but at all costs to keep the ASA's existence secret. Major General George Keegan, Director of Air Force Intelligence during the Vietnam War refused to pass any information to American pilots in combat. This created a huge sense of ill will between pilots and the intelligence agents, and the same as ill will existed between the combat units like the 11th ACR and the 'attached' ASA specialists in the field. After validating this ludicrous bureaucratic policy across branches of service it is no wonder that Jack was dismayed by his time in the Army and his sworn duty requiring him to unwittingly support the dynamics of the ASA/NSA 'greendoor syndrome', even if he did not hear these words himself while on active duty.MT There were a total a 269 American and enemy aircraft shot down in air-to-air combat over Vietnam during the entire war—201 in fights between the U.S. Air Force and North Vietnamese air force and just 68 in the U.S. Navy's air battles with the North Vietnamese. In those fights, the U.S. Air Force lost 64 aircraft and the Navy lost twelve. I wonder how many of those flights could have been prevented had it not been for the 'greendoor syndrome' policy. MT.

Milt: Did you ever return to the basecamp? Jack: I was at the base camp "Blackhorse" a few times but even there we were not allowed to mingle with the cavalry troopers due to our top-security clearance. My DEROS (date estimated return from overseas) was July 15th, but I received notice to ship out on July 8th. I jumped on a 'slick' (Huey UH-1 gunship) and flew to Ben Hoa. Then at the reception station for departure and I was amazed to witness the self-segregation of the troops anxiously awaiting to get aboard their flights back to 'the world'.

-Addressing Racism

Milt: There was friction between American troops, and claims of racism in Vietnam.

Jack: To answer this question, I'll have to digress a bit. Over the years, I've received messages stating that I was an unwitting racist. Being the recipient of such claims is perplexing; first that someone has taken the time to inform me what I am. I respect all people, but they've been 'drinking the Kool-Aid' a bit...I am not now, nor ever have been a racist. However, I am very prejudiced against prejudice people. To me racism is the supreme act of cowardice...represented by the attitude, 'I don't like you because you look different than I'. I was born into a military family, moving often; usually living in Army housing. I can't remember not being around blacks, browns, Asians, and other minorities of every persuasion.

Me and my black buddy Dicky (who bought the farm in Nam) used to cruise the streets of Los Angeles and the San Fernando Valley. Just him and me. We were friends, we were buddies, and had each other's backs. We knew we were different, but that was not important. I recall a time that Dickey saw a group of black guys on the corner…I think in Granada Hills. It was late in the evening, we were a bit drunk; and Dickey yelled out the window at the group, using the infamous "n" word…and ducked. The guys looked at me, yelled some physical impossibilities, and I floored the '57 Chevy and got away listening to Dickie laugh uproariously.

In Korea I had two blacks among the 10 men with which I served. Off base there was a black section as well as a white. Very rarely did a white visit black turf or versa vise. In Germany of course I had the run-in with the black CO, but wasn't there long enough to observe any racial stuff.

I went to Vietnam; attached to the 11th Armored Cavalry Regiment in 1968-1969. The war was not only against the Vietcong and NVA. I also witnessed the conflict between the black activists and the rednecks that was prevalent in all military units. The symbolisms of doing the 'rap and dap', 'Afro' haircuts, Afro picks, not shaving due to 'pseudo-folliculitis', blaring 'boom-boxes', rap vs. country music, 'peace symbols' and racial 'graffiti' irritated the black and white issues. Even though I had a couple black buddies in my unit; the racial tension was incredible, and confusing to me after my upbringing. Not all whites were rednecks; not all blacks were activists. Most probably recognized we were all military issue brothers. As discussed earlier, the closest I came to death was in May 1969, when my track was hit by an RPG (rocket propelled grenade) during a firefight near Loc Minh. The concussion knocked me out of the turret.

Stunned, and on the ground, I had no weapon, was not sure where I was, and as the fight raged around me two black soldiers from an adjoining track, ran out to risk their lives, and pulled me back into another track. I remembered July 9th as I was leaving country to go back to "the world" and discharge. Sitting in the air terminal at Bien Hoa; I kept my back to the wall and watched the groups of blacks watching the groups of whites. Nothing was said, but the glares were intense. I remember thinking; "I survived my tour, and certainly don't want to be wasted by a fellow American

Milt: It seems ironic that once the soldiers were separated from their respective units and were once again 'individuals', they voluntarily segregated themselves into racial groups. When in their military units, they had a bond to serve together and fight together regardless of racial identity.

Jack: Peer pressure played a role where black soldiers stayed together and did not mingle with the white soldiers at the air terminal. I did not have any prejudice in me, but I could sense the high tension between the two groups back in 1969.

Following my tour in Nam, and now a civilian, I got involved with a group of drug dealers. We were a pretty big outfit; and we looked like the United Nations...whites/blacks/browns/Asians. The only time I ever heard the "n" word was blacks using it frequently while talking with/arguing with one another.

A few years later I was arrested, tried, convicted and sentenced for ten years. I was converted to faith in Christ and the gospel while in jail. The first few years of my Christian life found me worshiping in essentially a black church in Oregon State Penitentiary. Most of the offenders in prison are black, and thus most of those inmates who choose to go to chapel are also people of color. They often led the services. When I got out of jail, I started going to church on the streets which was rather boring. For example, "Let's stand together and sing the first, second, and fourth stanzas of hymn number 356." What's the matter with the third verse?

Prison is easily survivable if you "do your own time." Which means no running with gangs; racial or otherwise. I was "discipled", though none of us knew that term, by a black guy who took me under his wing and, since he had been raised in the church, taught me Bible basics.

Since hitting the pavement, going to Bible school, and serving in youth and prison ministry full-time for forty plus years; I still rub shoulders with other "races" daily. I regularly preach at an all Korean/American camp every summer since 1988. I've spoken at an all Indian (Mar Thoma) camp several times and accepted for who I am as a person. When I look at any person, I see exactly that…a person, not color, not race. I try to recognize that every person I meet has God's stamp on him/her. I don't file them in a box based on their color. Red and yellow, black, brown and white, they (all) are precious in His sight. So, though I will never apologize for being an old, seasoned, white, conservative male; neither will I be silent if someone accuses me of being a racist in any form or setting.

Specialist 5th Class John "Jack" Hager left the military disappointed and disillusioned with the U.S. government and lack of leadership as well as unfilled potential for service to his country. The government 'power group' had also failed his expectations that included the 'greendoor syndrome' of bureaucratic failures on the battlefield. Colonel Millett's leadership by example had a positive influence on Jack while in ASA training, but then he was left to his own devices and future military leadership was non-existent. If there had been more leaders like Colonel Millett; I suggest that Jack's story may have had a different direction. So, Jack resorted to his old habits of drowning himself with alcohol, marijuana and drugs. "People do not determine their futures; they determine their habits; and their habits determine their future." Thus, Jack's search resumes for meaning in his life. (MT)

Chapter 5

Potential Unfulfilled –
Back in "The World"

Milt: Did you or your ASA crew receive commendations upon leaving Vietnam? Jack: Not to my knowledge. I lost touch with most of the guys; though I am still acquainted with one of our drivers who now lives in Arizona. And, none of my crew ever face any UCMJ charges or discipline either.

Milt: When you were released from active duty, were you required to sign a non-disclosure agreement on behalf of your top-secret duty for life? Jack: Yes, even before leaving the warzone I was taken into a tent with a Captain, as I remember it. He warned me to forget everything I knew/saw; and I signed a basic non-disclosure statement ensuring I'd not speak/write/mention the classified details not only of my time in Nam, but all my time in the Agency.

Milt: We will be exploring the many travels, jobs, experiences and changes in your life over four decades following your service in Vietnam. Knowing a bit of what is ahead, I am wondering if you might have post-traumatic stress disorder? Jack: If so, I've not been diagnosed with PTSD, nor have I self-diagnosed with PTSD. I've never had any flashbacks, nightmares or night sweats. I was simply an alcoholic and hooked on drugs. I simply didn't care about anything. I learned how to handle a hangover...just remain drunk. I was an opportunist and stayed mostly in the fog all the time. By 1969 I was filled with hate for America for how bureaucrats conducted the war in Vietnam and how the Johnson Administration and bureaucrats reacted with apathy to the Pueblo capture. We sacrificed 83 service members on the Pueblo and lost all the intel equipment, and did nothing about it. Our leadership position in the world was squandered in Korea, Germany, and now in Vietnam and I was an eyewitness to these failures. We were told not to go into Cambodia or Laos to pursue the enemy and destroy them in their sanctuary. America did not fight the war to win and that bothered me. We sacrificed lives of soldiers in Vietnam for nothing once again.

Milt: Where did your flight land back in 'the world'? Jack: Landing at Travis AFB was memorable. We were kept on the plane buying time for the Air Police to keep the crowd away from us. The protesters were prevalent. The protestors were against the soldiers as well as the country. I remember this gorgeous blond gal yelling: 'How many babies did you kill….how many babies did you kill? This grizzly Marine behind me sarcastically yelled back at her; "Only as many as I could eat"! That didn't stop her from yelling. Yet, there were older men with red jackets on who were Veterans trying to welcome us home because they understood the hurt. The Vietnam protestors were against we, the soldiers who served to protect their right to protest. Ironically, today the protestors were against the Afghanistan war, but not against the soldiers….that's the difference.

I out-processed at Presidio and took a room in San Francisco. I went to my parent's home in Richmond California where my dad was now working for the Social Security Administration to visit them. I knocked on the door and they said, "What are you doing here?" A bit stunned, I said; 'I'd like to say "Hi". They then said; "You're not welcome here", so, I left and never returned. The moral to this welcome home event is….'you can't miss what you never had'. I can never remember being loved, never living in a home that cared, and now it was coming back at me after I returned home for combat in Vietnam.

• Once again, a civilian, John "Jack" Hager reverted to his old value system in his own words…"I simply didn't care." The power groups of 'police and courts' would play the major role in this phase of Jack's life. Jack's unlimited potential has been on hold for twenty+ years at this point in his life. (MT)

Chapter 6

Downward Spiral to Rock Bottom.

I applied to be a dispatcher for the City of Richmond with the police department and almost got that job as a 'top 3' finalist. Then I saw an ad in the paper that read: Have you recently been discharged from the military, do you have a security clearance? Come and see us. It was 'Global Associates', that reviewed my DD 214 and hired me to go to Kwajalein. I had no idea what Kwajalein was. They offered me 11 months of duty on this Pacific Island Atoll and following that tour, I could take an all-expense paid vacation anywhere in the world as long as I returned to Kwaj. I was hired based on my clearance and gave me the job title of radar surveillance technician. I flew to Hawaii and then the Kwajalein to my spartan barracks on the atoll. I virtually did nothing for a 'tax free' job. I worked 5 days a week and could volunteer for weekend duty at extra pay. The ocean water was deep blue and so clear that when flying over the area I could see the sunken ships and aircraft wreckages from WWII. I was twenty-two and got bored with doing nothing while ripping off the American taxpayers working for this contractor. There were only men on this job site as well. I was frustrated, quit and flew to Hawaii where I was introduced to a new level of criminal activity.

[Kwajalein is the 14th largest coral atoll as measured by area of enclosed water. Comprising 97 islands and islets, it has a land area of 6.33 mi², and surrounds one of the largest lagoons in the world, with an area of 839 mi². The average height above sea level for all the islands is about me 5 ft 11 in. On February 1, 1944, Kwajalein was the target of the most concentrated bombardment of the Pacific War. An estimated 36,000 shells from naval ships and ground artillery on a nearby islet struck Kwajalein. American B-24 Liberator bombers aerially bombarded the island, adding to the destruction. The conditions in the makeshift labor camp on Kwajalein islet were such that the U.S. Navy administering the atoll decided to relocate these Islanders to nearby Ebeye, an islet only three islands to the north of Kwajalein and accessible by a short boat ride or walk over the reef at low tide. Nuclear refugees from the atolls irradiated by the American tests were also moved to Ebeye. Radar installations, optics, telemetry, and communications equipment, which are used for ballistic missile and missile-interceptor testing, and for space operations support is why Jack got the job with his security clearance. Kwajalein island hosts the $914 million Space Fence radar, which tracks satellites and orbital debris. Kwajalein has one of five ground stations used in controlling the RTS range, which also assist in the operation of the Global Positioning System (GPS) navigation system.] (MT)

I met a girl at a bar who was a stewardess. She also worked for some guys smuggling drugs. We started living together and she soon introduced me to these guys. They basically interviewed me and hired me to work on the West Coast, primarily transporting marijuana and weapons up and down the coast.

The details are unimportant, and I don't want to glamorize the lifestyle by going into detail. Suffice to say I had a lot of money and a lot of stuff. Inside, I was pretty bored; but I couldn't reveal that to anyone. Shortly after Thanksgiving of 1973, my woman wanted to travel from our West Coast home to Texas where her parents lived. By that time, I had accumulated a lot of cash and the cops were getting better at figuring out who was doing what…a couple of my associates had been arrested recently, so I decided it was time to get out of the business and make a permanent move to Texas.

Oh, I should point out that I had a "straight" job as a Greyhound station manager. A couple years previous I had seen a commercial on TV, "Go Greyhound, and leave the driving to us."

I had the genius idea of a few of us getting jobs at certain stations, and thus being able to load a suitcase full of weed, say, in Portland Oregon, monitor it through Redding, California and then on to either San Francisco or Los Angeles. It worked pretty well, but I did my baggage boy duties so well I was promoted to dispatcher, then a guy asked me to manage a small station.

Thus, when we took off for Texas, I emptied the safe of the station, knowing we wouldn't be back. On December 3 I was in a bar/club in San Angelo playing pool. Around 7pm my lady said we should go back and check on our kid, who we'd left with a babysitter. I was fine with that, but too toasted to drive, so I told her to drive as I slid in the passenger seat.

As she pulled out of the club she said, "Jack, we picked up a cop." I glanced over my shoulder and could make out a cop car behind us. I advised her just to chill and go a little more than the speed limit. There were no drugs in the car, my gun was at the hotel.

A few minutes later several cop cars turned on their lights/sirens. She pulled over. One of the cops said, on a bull horn, "You, riding shotgun…open the door, slide out on your face, and don't move."

I looked at all the guns and decided he had a great idea. I exited the car, lay on the ground; and soon a shotgun was placed to my neck while another officer patted me down to ensure I wasn't carrying. I was pulled to a standing position, and then I was read my rights. They did not arrest the girl with me. I was taken and booked into the Tom Greene County Jail.

The next day I was indicted on several charges: most from Oregon, a couple from California, and federal charges. I had to stay in Texas for a few weeks awaiting extradition. At this point I wasn't sure who was going to get me first…Oregon, California, or the Feds.

Later California dropped the charges, and I was told the feds elected not to prosecute. I need to point out that the feds interviewed me on a few occasions both in Texas and Oregon. The substance of those conversations will not and cannot be revealed. Cooperation seemed to be the sensible thing for me to do, and that cooperation was "rewarded" with dropped charges.

A couple weeks after I was arrested a major incident took place that was going to set the stage for the biggest moments of my life. In an unannounced inspection the guards found drugs in our cell block. The fact they found drugs is not unique; drugs are easier to get in jail/prison than they are on the street…any jail, any prison.

The unique thing was they actually punished us…they removed the books, magazines, weights, games…everything…except what the courts declared they could not remove…the religious stuff.

So, all we had was a small pile of books and Bibles. Back then I was dumber than I am now, and I thought "religion" and "Christianity" were synonymous. All I knew was that I was a man and I did the crime and thus could do the time and didn't need any religious hocus pocus.

But after a couple days of having nothing to do, I examined the pile of books a little more thoroughly. I had never read the Bible before, didn't need it now. But I did discover a small paperback book with the word "prison" in the title. (I will not reveal the title for it is loaded with what I learned was bad teaching).

I had been in jail a few times, but never prison. So, I picked up the book not in some search for God or meaning, but to gather information regarding prison. At that time, it was reasonable to think I was going to be locked up for a long, long time; and I wanted as much heads up as I could. The book told the story of an alcoholic WWII veteran, his run-ins with the law, his arrest, and subsequent decision to be a Christian.

As I read his story, I noted he kept quoting Bible verses. Though I was still operating out of boredom rather than a quest for knowledge, I found a Bible and began to read. At this point I am 26 years old. I have never been in church except for weddings and funerals. I had no concept who Jesus Christ was, what a Christian was, what the Bible was about.

I was not an atheist. I knew there had to be a "first primary cause." I knew there had to be a Creator. But if there was a Creator, I was the created; and as such I was accountable to the Creator…and I did not want to be accountable to anyone. I recall a time in high school when a few friends and I went to the beach late one night to drink and hang out. Laying on the Malibu beach we looked up at a star-filled sky. I did not know the Bible says, "the heavens declare the glory of God." The heavens were just doing their job.

And as a group of semi-drunk teens gazed, we started talking about the big questions – Who am I? How did I get here? Where am I going? I remember my buddy Rich said, "You know what, I think the Martians planted us like a science project." We chuckled, but, hey, could be. But where did the Martians come from? Where did Mars come from? Where did anything come from?

So again, we bounced back to the idea of a creator. None of us could believe that long, long time ago nothing got in nothing and made a something. Evolution made no sense, because at some point there was nothing...so how did anything "evolve" out of nothing? I don't recall what ended the discussion (probably too much Jack Daniels).

Fast forward to early January in a Texas jail cell. And there I am...for the first time, reading a Bible. I somehow made it through the Old Testament and into the four gospels (Matthew, Mark, Luke, John). At this point I am introduced to Jesus Christ.

Again, I am not "looking for God," I am not looking for a way out. I am simply bored and reading the Bible because there was basically nothing else to read. Looking back, I think the first thing that attracted me to Jesus was the observation that He never hammered the hookers, the prostitutes, the thieves, the 'low lifes'.

No, the only people He rebuked were the religious folks...the people who thought they had favor with God because they had their list of do's and don't and were striving to be obedient to those man-made rules. Jesus was definitely not "politically-correct" or "sensitive" with those religious folks. That seemed rather cool to me.

As I continued reading, I became more captivated with Christ and the story. Unbeknownst to me (and without my permission!), God's Holy Spirit was using His inspired Word to convict me of sin, righteousness, and judgment. As I contemplated His life, His death, and His alleged (to me) resurrection; I remember thinking, "this is science fiction" and I tossed the Bible across the cellblock.

But I could not get Jesus out of my head. Again, now I understand that was the convicting power of God's Spirit evidencing His incredible love by convincing me of the reality of Christ and the good news...the gospel.

On January 30, 1974, I was "born-again," "saved," or...the term more legitimate in my mind – "converted." There was no "repeat-after-me-prayer", there was no chaplain; there was simply an incredibly lost sinner (that would be me); and an incredibly loving God.

I don't have a clue what I said, how I prayed, or anything else. I know at some level I acknowledged that I was a cosmic rebel against a Holy God, and somehow understood that this incredibly awesome God provided a way for me to be made right with Him...and that way was the substitutionary death of Jesus. I saw that Jesus lived the life I could not live; and died the death I should have died.

In short, I did what John 3.16 says, "God so loved the world that He gave His only begotten Son so that whoever BELIEVES on Him would not perish, but would have eternal life."

Important to note that the English language is weak. The word "believe" does not mean the same thing as when I used to say I believed in Santa Claus, or I believed the United States could never make a mistake, or I believed (and staked my life on my belief) that I was the best drug dealer/thief on the West Coast and I'd never got busted.

Nope..I found out Santa wasn't real; I learned the US could make a horrific mistake in a place called Vietnam; and when those cops turned on their lights, I knew I wasn't as slick as I thought I was. No, "belief" in Jesus (and in the original Greek) means to trust, to rely on.

I trusted Christ. Forty plus years later I still trust Christ.

I am not going to heaven because I don't smoke marijuana anymore. I am not going to heaven because I don't rip off people anymore. I am not going to heaven because I don't do those things anymore…I am going to heaven because "Jesus paid it all, all to Him I owe, sin had left a crimson stain, but He washed it right as snow."

I know some of you readers don't buy into the 'Faith in Christ' thing. I respect that; and only ask that you consider Jesus, not His kids. We screw it up all the time, we are not the representatives we should be…so I ask you, before you blow off Jesus, read the Gospel of John for yourself…just to check it/Him out.

Milt: During this 'conversion' as described above; how long were you in the Texas jail? Jack: I spent about two months in the jail, being interviewed by various law enforcement types from different states as well as the Feds. Then the Oregon county sheriff flew to Texas to extradite me back to Oregon primarily for stealing the Greyhound money from their safe. The sheriff treated me with respect and said he was not going to cuff me, there was no statute of limitations on escape, nowhere to run and he said: "Just behave yourself and come with me." I was back in Oregon to audition my orange jumpsuit.

I was in the general population with other inmates. A couple times I was threatened by the interrogators in an attempt to have me confess to crimes that I did not commit. It was basically a game… they held out carrots of dropped charges while trying to gather more information on other operations with which I was involved. Though I would not call myself a snitch (since most of the guys had already been arrested) I did – sort of – cooperate with the investigators.

Milt: Did you go through withdrawal from the drugs when in jail? Jack: No, I've never experienced any withdrawal symptoms. I was in a constant buzz, and in jail it was easier to get drugs than being on the street. The 'trustees' and guards were great sources of drugs.

Milt: Did you have a jury trial? Jack: No, I told my court appointed attorney that I did everything I was charged with, and I plead 'nola contendre' which means 'no contest'. The judge originally sentenced me to 10 years in prison; but my attorney pleaded my good service in the Army and the judge reduced it to 3 years. At that time California and the feds still had charges hanging on me (that would be dropped within a year); so I think the sentencing judge thought he could be lenient with me knowing (in his mind) that I'd end up doing California time and maybe federal time.

- Darkness of hopelessness, uncertainty, cheating, drug addiction and theft led to incarceration, extradition and conviction to serve time in the Oregon State Prison. The downward spiral to hit rock bottom was the turning point to reverse the imprinted values of his early life when Jack's SEE (significant emotional event) reading the Bible for the first time resulted in Jack discovering the 'authentic power' of Jesus Christ. The former power groups of parents, peers, police and courts, government, employers and physicians all went to the wayside and replaced by the 'only authentic power of Jesus Christ' that penetrated Jack's being and now we'll see if Jack achieves his unlimited potential. (MT)

Chapter 7

'SEE' to Jesus Christ as the only Authentic Power (Being Tested)

Jack: Most people have no idea about the real life in prison. Anyone can read textbooks, novels, watch movies on TV, or watch documentaries on prison life; but until they actually experience checking into prison, they really do not understand. Within the first few days on incarceration, you will be tested by someone or some group to "test" your mettle. They want to know 'how much heart' you had. It was the 3rd or 4th day in prison while walking in the yard that I had this guy walk up to me and say: "Hey blondie". I was put on high alert for what was about to follow. He proceeded to tell me what he was going to do to me in very graphic language to include rape. I said: "No, you are not, you dirt face"! With all the force I could muster I hit him and he staggered just a bit, grinned, turned and walked away. I had 'passed the test' and the rest of the inmates knew I had the 'heart' to stand my ground and defend myself. It is a right-of-passage faced by every inmate in a maximum-security prison and to shrink from it only makes your prison life more miserable each and every day.

Milt: I've thought a bit about your prison time and terms such as isolation, loneliness, uncertainty, fear, hopelessness, and intensity come to mind. Jack: I think it is like childbirth. I will never know what it is like to give birth; though I've been in the room as my wife delivered our two sons. I just haven't "been there, done that." In that sense prison is like combat; unless and until you are there to hear/smell/taste/experience you have no clue. What is prison like? A poem expresses it well:

"At night I lay here staring, at these cold, cold walls of steel.
And realize the walls reflect, just how they make me feel.
You see those words scratched on the walls,
Like "love" and "hate" and "die,"
They were put there for a reason,
Yes, the walls can tell you why.
You see those little runs of paint,
Collected over all the years?
They remind me of the lonesome nights,
It's strange they look like tears.
And now that I have met you walls,
I know this much is real;
There is nothing quite as lonely,
As your cold, cold walls of steel."

Milt: You became a different person in prison than you were just a couple months earlier on the street. Now, you see your former self with the other prisoners in the Oregon State Prison. How did you fit in? Jack: The prison was in Salem at Oregon's only maximum security prison. I was blessed that the overall prison population was not huge at that time, thus I was in a one-man cell throughout my incarceration. Mostly in D-365; "D" Block (of 5 blocks), 3rd floor (of

5), 65th cell. The guy in the cell to my left happened to be an African American guy who was doing life without parole. The prison rumor was that he had multiple murder charges. One of the unwritten rules of prison is that you never ask anyone what they are in for; nor do you volunteer to tell anyone what charges led to your imprisonment.

The prisoner in the cell to my right was a white guy who apparently had never done anything wrong in his life…til he came home to discover his wife in bed with the next door neighbor; and the story was he killed them both.

That's the reality of prison life first time offenders are mixed in with guys doing life-on-the-installment-plan (three years here, out for a while, two years there etc). So, a low-key drug dealer will be housed with rapists, child-molesters, strong-arm men, murderers etc. Then society expect them to come out different. The cliché of prison being a school for advanced criminal learning is a cliché because it is true.

Most prisons offer a variety of educational opportunities. I seized every one I could take. But many of the inmates do nothing to advance themselves as it is seen by the herd as "cooperating with the man." I can't imagine doing time not knowing how to read, but functional illiteracy is very common and, again, most of the offenders don't avail themselves of the available help.

The stories of drugs, rapes, murders etc, behind the walls may be exaggerated, but such things do happen. But the most horrible thing about the American prison system is that the system programs inmates to fail.

When I checked into OSP (Oregon State Prison), I spent a week or so taking tests…aptitude, intelligence, square peg round hole etc. Not because I was "me," but because I was 36403 coming into the system. I was interviewed by staff psychiatrists, a couple grad students at Oregon State University, and a chaplain.

At the end of this in-processing, I appeared in front of the parole board, as every inmate does. The theory is the board members look at all the data and then come up with a "program" for the offender to follow. It may be to get a GED, go to drug classes, get involved with victim reconciliation programs, etc. The carrot held out is that if the offender follows through on these "recommendations" the board will look more favorably on him when he appears before the board down the road.

So, what is the programming to fail? Simply this…I don't question the ethics or commitment of board members; but they operate from the theory that man is "good," so if man goes "bad" they must come up with a reason. The board told me that the reason I was in prison was because of the bad attitude I had because of my experiences in the military, particularly Vietnam.

What have they just done? They've told me "it's not my fault." They may cite another prisoners' race; family break up, molestation, etc, as causal agents. Certainly environment contributes, but we are responsible beings who make our own choices…and then our choices make us.

As a Christian I know man is inherently "bad" because of sin. Can an inmate go "straight" without a religious system of belief? Absolutely. Does converting to Christ guarantee an inmate will never return? Absolutely not. We continue to have that incredible power of choice. And instead of encouraging offenders to take personal responsibility for their actions, the establishment provides an "excuse."

It leads to prisoners feeling and acting like a five-year-old – "It's not my fault! Jimmie did it. Drugs did it. My parent's divorce did it." NO! You did it, and unless and until a person owns their responsibility they cannot change it, with or without Christ. The Oregon State Penitentiary is a maximum-security prison that sits on 194 acres in the heart of Salem, just north of Mill Creed on State Street. Twenty-two acres of the facility ae surrounded by concrete, twenty-five-foot-high wall that extends fifteen feet into the ground, with ten armed-guard towers.

Milt: Was there a routine in prison? Jack: There was a metal bunk, a stool and a sink in my cell; it was maximum security. There was a radio built into the cell. I woke about 0530 hours and they varied the times for meals to avoid setting a routine and keep the prisoners off balance. They'd conduct a head count, go to breakfast, do another headcount. Then open select doors for those who had jobs, classes to attend, or counseling. The other prisoners stayed in their cells for a couple more hours before being let out for 'yard time'. I'd go to my prison job until around 11:30 and back to my cell for another head count, then to lunch, followed by another headcount when back in the cells. Afternoon routine was the same with continuous headcounts when any movement of prisoners to activities or evening meal took place. We'd fill out request forms that listed our wishes for work, school, educational reading and all potential activities. Then the forms were reviewed and approved or disapproved. I've visited many prisons since Oregon and it was already progressive in the 1970's. There was an 'honor farm' for livestock and garden foods all grown and tended by the prisoners. The food was excellent and fresh and nothing to gripe about. We had plastic ware and styrofoam cups to discourage fashioning weapons in prison.

Milt: Did you form any friendships in prison? Jack: To survive in prison you had to know your surroundings at all times. Or, as Colonel Patton would thunder, "Stay alert, stay alive!" You did your own time or you could identify with groups/gangs. If you hang with one of the gangs, you do their time in addition to yours.

Like Vietnam, the night was the worst. The noise was amazing…like 500 radio stations on 500 different signals all going full blast. Guys yelling to other men about killing/raping, whatever. There were some inmates in prison who should have been in the state hospital. They were always legally mediated into a virtual comatose state. Really sad.

There were a couple guys I knew from the street, and I kept away from them. I just did not want to be seen associating with anyone. I did go to Chapel and met a few guys there and was mentored by a black guy educated in deep Christian heritage. I learned how to read the Bible from him. I can understand why anyone can go to prison once; but I just don't get it when guys go back and forth to prison. The 70% recidivism boggles my mind.

Milt: In Vietnam, you had a 'short-timers calendar', did you also have one in prison? Jack: No, I did not have a short-timer calendar in prison like we had in Vietnam to make our DEROS. You knew that a third of your sentence would be cut off as long as you were on good behavior. So, it was the strategy to "do your own time", not get involved with a gang, clique or anything that distracted you from parole and release.

Milt: Did you get mail in jail? Jack: I got mail, because early on in my cell I wrote to the judge who sentenced me back in Oregon. I encouraged him to throw out current practices of juvenile justice. I told him that if a teenager were picked up for an offense; that they should send him / her to jail or prison for a period of time to teach them that actions have consequences, instead of the proverbial slap on the wrist and yelled threats.

I also included in my letter the fact that I had become a Christian. For some reason the judge gave the letter to the local newspaper. The paper cut out my Christianity, but published the rest of the letter. UPI picked it up and it must have appeared in a lot of papers, because all of a sudden I was getting lots and lots of mail; to the point the mail clerks hated me.

Much of the mail was from religious people…varying from Christian to Muslim to Christian Science trying to get me to see the light. A lot of the mail was from desperate women who wanted to get married… to anyone.

Milt: Were there any 'special' letters you received? Jack: Yes; Mr. and Mrs. Gene West wrote me from Newhall, California and they had a house next door to the high school from which I graduated. They saw the original letter and wrote me very early on in the process. I'd hate to think where my life would have ended up if it had not been for them taking the time to write to me in prison. We corresponded for the entire time I was behind bars. The first time I went before the parole board they gave me 'the flop'…and that was expected.

The next time I appeared the board said they believed I was "rehabilitated" and was ready to be released. But because of the publicity my case had received they wanted me to go to another state, a system called "reciprocal parole." I applied to California and was accepted, with my brother being the person with whom I would stay when released.

Milt: Tenacity comes to my mind when describing you. Where you tenacious in this transitory phase in life? Jack: Upon parole I flew to L.A. and stayed with my brother for a few weeks. Made some dumb choices, then decided to get serious in my faith. I walked to Newhall, California where the Wests lived. As I walked into the driveway Mr. West was under the hood of a car; he looked up and said, "We've been waiting for you."

These folks had a teenage daughter, and all they knew about me was what I told them. In some ways they were foolish to offer me hospitality, but they walked their faith. They attended the First Baptist Church of Newhall, and I soon got a job there as what I called a "Minister of Sanitation," otherwise known as a Janitor.

The church foolishly wanted me to be the youth leader. I think they felt the token ex-con would draw a lot of kids. By God's grace I took the position. I had no clue what I was doing, but I leaned into God for guidance and the group grew. The church had a k-6th grade school, and on Easter week 1977 they told me to wash all the windows while the kids were on vacation, and assigned a teenager to help me. His name was Billy Bob Maxim. After the first day he asked if I'd speak at his "Youth For Christ" club.

I probably said, "What's a youth for Christ club?" Billy Bob told me that his parents were raised in Kansas City and attended all the youth programs of Kansas City 'Youth For Christ', to include their camps. The parents were so blessed by their camp experience that they sent Billy Bob and his younger brother to the week-long camp. Among other things they learned that YFC had Bible clubs in many, many middle/junior/high schools.

So, Billy came back and started a club. I spoke, and if memory serves there were about fifty teens at that first meeting. Running the rapidly expanding youth group, speaking and helping with the YFC club, and even preaching a couple Sunday morning services revealed to me my love for the Word of God and for preaching/teaching the Bible. I felt "called" to do so vocationally, but I had no clue how that would happen.

A guy named Jerry Johnston came to our town. Jerry was probably 19 or 20 at the time. He had been converted through a YFC program, and was basically a public relations guy for Kansas City YFC as well as for a fledging Bible school called Liberty University....Yeah, Jerry Falwell's school. I got to meet Jerry after he preached, and he told me of a Bible institute run by Kansas City Youth For Christ and he encouraged me to apply.

It was attractive...it was inexpensive, only a year long, and was basically three hours a day in the Bible, an hour a day in principles of youth ministry; and several hours daily helping in the various aspects of the large YFC ministry. I did apply. Dr Al and Vidy Metsker were the founders of KCYFC, as well as the President of the Bible institute. They also decided on accepting the applicants. Several years later Vidy told me that she and Al looked over my application, then looked at each other and wondered if they should take a chance on a guy recently released from prison and still on parole. After much thought and prayer, they decided to give me a chance...a decision for which I am forever grateful.

Milt: You now have 'people wealth' as a resource, rather than alcohol, drugs, and cash as a resource. Jack: Well, what I had, and have... is an ongoing relationship with my Creator through the Lord Jesus Christ. No longer did I see people as projects to take advantage of; no longer was I looking out for my own best interests. I was beginning to learn, as I am still learning, how to live as a servant of Christ and a server of people. The genuine Christian life is not as complicated as we often make it out to be. It's really pretty simple – Love God; love people. All too often Christians separate themselves from other Christians for stupid reasons...It seems many are more in love with their denomination or their pet doctrine than they are in love with Jesus

When I first got to prison the chaplain asked me if I was Protestant or Catholic. At the time I wasn't even sure what each word meant; and had no idea...but I did recall my dog tags said "Protestant" so that is what I identified as. The chaplain then asked me about my "religious life" and I told him I had been saved in jail in Texas.

He shook his head and said something like, "We don't get emotional here," and he handed me a book dealing with transactional analysis. I didn't know much about anything, but I knew I was not on the same page as this guy. Thankfully he never preached in prison. Each Sunday a different group would come in; one Sunday it would be a sort of Christian rock band, the next Sunday a representative of the Gideon Bible ministry, the next Sunday a missionary home on furlough etc. We got a steady dose of "come to Jesus" sermons, but for those of us who were already followers of Christ there was not a lot of teaching, or discipleship.

I did attend a Bible study run by a Baptist preacher. These weekly meetings were a great source of teaching for me. I also availed myself of several correspondence courses, for which I am grateful.

(Billy Graham served as the first full-time evangelist of the Youth for Christ ministry in the mid-1940s. Torrey Johnson, the founder of Youth for Christ, called a young Graham to take over one of his radio programs in Chicago. At the time, Billy was serving as pastor of a small Baptist church in Western Springs, Illinois. After several months on the air, Johnson offered Billy Graham an even greater opportunity – to kick off the first night of "Chicagoland's Youth for Christ" meetings and, eventually, become the first vice-president of Youth for Christ International.)

Milt: In your previous life, you likely never stood in front of groups of people and offered your advice, guidance, counsel, and opinions. Were you comfortable with this new role?

Jack: In prison there was a program called "Masters Men" which was like the Toastmasters Club. We'd attend and draw slips of paper with topics to speak on in an extemporaneous manner. I was getting on my feet in front of small groups for the first time to speak publicly. Then one week, the leader said: "Jack, you'll now be making a 15 minute sermon at the next gathering." Wow, that was a challenge, but for my first time I prepared by studying the Bible, drawing lessons from my research and sharing that with others. It built my confidence and taught me a 'research/speaking process' for effective communications in front of groups.

The training and practical experience I gained going to the KC school ("Christ Unlimited Bible Institute" – which sadly does not exist anymore) was invaluable, and that training and experience colors my ministry these forty plus years later.

After graduation I went on staff of KC-YFC as an evangelist. I spoke three or four times a week at Bible clubs and churches, and began my camp speaking ministry shortly thereafter.

Milt: You have been in multiple situations from one-on-one, small groups, school assemblies, church sermons, Bible clubs, civic organizations, jails and prisons. Which of these settings is most and least stressful for you? Jack: Stress is not a bad word. Since 1978 people of all ages have often asked, "Jack, are you scared to preach in front of people." The answer – YES! The Word of God says, "Not many should become teachers, my brothers, because you know that we will receive a stricter judgment." (James 3.1) I don't pretend to understand all that verse entails, but if I am standing up professing to be speaking for the Lord, I had better have some level of stress/fear... elsewise I am relying on my own "clever" speaking 'teachniques' rather than clinging to the Spirit of God. That said, my favorite place to preach is prison – the audience already knows they are screwed. My least favorite place? Christian schools...wherein most of the audience thinks they've heard everything and know everything.

In just 34 years, John "Jack" Hager had gone through eight phases in his life; (1) value imprinting at age 11 as a 'manipulator', (2) disappointing search for discipline and leadership in military service, (3) back in "the world" and downward spiral, (4) incarceration and loss of freedom, (5) finding the Lord, and conversion, (6) surviving prison life, (7) dropping his 'façade' to become trusted, and responsible, (8) proving himself in the eyes of the Lord. Now the greatest challenge is the next phase (9) ahead for Jack to serve Jesus Christ as a husband, parent, and example to follow as a mentor, teacher, counselor, and leader. Most people go through life with 'unlimited potential' but never realized. Jack is now converting his unlimited potential into a productive life, with no hidden agenda. (MT)

Chapter 8

Life Changes with the Love of My Life

Milt: How did you come to travel to Kansas City in August, 1977 to become part of Youth for Christ? Jack: As mentioned earlier, there was a young evangelist who was attending Jerry Falwell's Liberty College and was also linked to Kansas City Youth For Christ. His name is Jerry Johnston, and he introduced me to CUBI while I was still on parole. Reverend Alfred Earl "Al" Metsker and his wife Vidy founded the Youth for Christ and CUBI to work in a cooperative manner. Metsker and his wife were the admissions officers for CUBI; and years later I was told that on their way driving to Edgerton, Missouri they debated my application. They took a chance on me at age 30, and I was accepted as a fulltime student which was another major change in my future life. I flew from Los Angeles with $30.00 in my pocket along with a small suitcase and no place to live. I was picked up early in the morning at the airport and taken to the Youth for Christ headquarters where arrangements were made for my temporary living quarters. I asked if I could use a typewriter to crank out a couple letters. The guy in the cubicle across from me heard me pounding on the typewriter skills and was so impressed by my proficiency that he asked if I wanted a job as a clerk. Then I was taken to Circle-C ranch that the Metsker's owned for temporary quarters until I found a permanent place to stay.

[The story of Kansas City Youth For Christ is a love story-a three-fold love story of its founders, Dr. Al and Vidy Metsker: their individual love for the Lord, their love for each other, and the love they shared for teenagers. This is the story of the unwavering faith, intense determination, boundless vision, faithful obedience, contagious enthusiasm and personal integrity of a man and woman who were willing to put themselves at God's disposal. "God specializes in using nobodies," was Al's explanation for what happened during their 50 years of ministry together. – Publisher Dr. Metsker founded the organization in 1943. He also founded television station KYFC and the LIGHT House Home for Pregnant Girls in Kansas City; the Circle C Ranch, Edgerton in Johnson County; and the L-Bar-C Ranch, La Cygne, Kan. He helped establish and was past president of the Calvary Bible College, Belton. He was past president of the Youth Evangelism Association and served on the boards of directors of the National Religious Broadcasters Association and Youth for Christ International. He received honorary doctorates from John Brown University, Siloam Springs, Ark., and Liberty University, Lynchburg, Va. He was born in Greenwood County, Kan., and moved to this area in 1940.]

Milt: Did you develop a niche in your speaking style?

Jack: I came to know a dear family in Union Star, Missouri (the home of Arnold the pig, who may be familiar to readers of a certain age) and we had a great friendship. I spent a lot of time at their home, when one day one of the daughters asked if I'd speak at their high school about my life experiences.

Milt: What were the names of this family? The Scott family…they had four daughters, all of whom are still my honorary (to me) sisters. One suggested that I tell my story to the students and the invitation was extended to me. I prepared a presentation that stressed personal responsibility. I did not hold back anything of my past and you could hear a pin drop on the floor. I told the students that they could become a thief like myself and make lots of money…. but you may go to prison and pay the consequences. You could 'sleep around'…but, you may get pregnant and pay the price. You can use drugs, steal, sell drugs all you want, it's your choice….but, there will be consequences.

I emphasized that every student must take responsibilities for their own actions. The system says that 'it's not your fault' that you're pregnant, that you use drugs, that you sell drugs or that you steal. The system repeats over and over again that it is not your fault and these young people are victims. I bring reality to the equation, and some hopefully realize that the only one to blame is yourself. I was invited to a Catholic High School in Kansas City the next week; followed by school after school with more school assembly speaking engagements. Then the model turned to conducting the assembly for one hour and staying in school in classrooms answering the student's questions. This lasted for seven years with sometimes two or three assemblies every day. The post critiques were always positive and often stated my assemblies were the best that were ever heard. After one assembly, while being escorted to a classroom, a student stopped me and said: "I don't agree with anything you said, but at least I understood what you said." That critique was very important and told me I was doing the right thing.

When in front of an audience, I tell them that I am there to talk about something they think they know a lot about, but in reality, they know nothing about. I am told that I don't look like an ex-con and I tell them that everyone has potential to go to prison, everyone has potential to become a pastor; but it comes down to personal responsibility and making good choices to succeed. At the conclusion of each event, I am always told that they have never heard a speaker like me. I don't think I have a 'canned speech', just an honest approach and I'm not running a game like I did as a criminal and con-man. Now I say: "Tell me how I can serve you."

Milt: Jack, you mentioned 'transactional analysis' a couple of time as proposed methods, techniques, and style suggested to you in ministry. As I understand TA is as described below: [TA was developed in the mid-20th century by psychiatrist Eric Berne (1910-1970). Its models are constantly evolving. Transactional Analysis is a collection of concepts that can help you better understand yourself and others. With it you can improve your communication skills. For example, to better resolve a conflict. With its comprehensible concepts and tools, it gives you opportunities to lead a more self-determined life. People are okay Communication is free and open: Every human being has the ability to think. The model is decision-oriented Every work is based on a contract / agreement: It can increase self-awareness. It promotes personal reflection. It helps people find more effective ways to communicate. It can help eliminate unhelpful thoughts, feelings, and actions.] Do you agree with the TA approach in ministry communications style?

Jack: Nope. I think there are things to be gleaned from such topics… to include psychology, psychiatry, various types of counseling… but in order to be true to my faith my reliance is on the Word of God, and God Himself. As has been said, "work like it's all up to you; pray like it's all up to God." Any speaker (regardless of faith or topic) should learn his/her own style. Too many try to copy a gifted communicator, instead of finding their own voice, their own style, their own quirks.

Milt: You married at age thirty-five.

Jack: I met Jane Elizabeth Francis in 1981. She was going to Bible school at CUBI, in Kansas City. The first time Jane saw me she thought I was the camp janitor. Then, that night she saw me as the camp speaker in front of the group. She was the roommate of the girl I was dating…I can't even remember her name. Jane joined us all the time going out to eat or to the movies, and called me "grandpa". In the fall of 1981, we were on a group trip to Steubenville, Ohio where I was invited to preach. On that trip, I realized that Jane and I were in love and I broke the news to the other girl. I was booked doing speaking engagements and school assemblies at that time and constantly on the road. We got married on Nov., 27th 1982, in Massachusetts and went to Niagara Falls for the honeymoon.

The unique thing about my relationship with Jane is hugely important…she was the first girl (since I was about 13) that I was friends with before I was anything else with. I tell young people that it is wise to first become friends with your future partner, and then that cements the love. It is essential to have much in common to keep the trust and lines of communications flowing. Jane was born in 1962 and fifteen years younger than me. She said that she thought I was younger, and I thought she was older than she was.

Milt: As a married couple, did the two of you have a plan for the future?

Jack: Not really, we kept busy with the school assemblies and other speaking engagements while on staff of KCYFC, and then the Lord led us to work with a youth ministry in Phillipsburg, Kansas for two years. Then we served with Headwaters Christian Youth in Rhinelander, Wisconsin for a couple years.

Milt: What prompted the move to Rhinelander, Wisconsin? Was that in 1984?

Jack: Not all readers will understand this, but God prompted the move. Our firstborn son Josiah was born in Phillipsburg, Kansas on 2/13/1984 and Joel was born in Rhinelander, Wisconsin on 10/22 1986. Because of our work schedules always being on the move, we decided to home school the children and took them on our travels as part of their education. After a couple years in Wisconsin, I was offered a position with Family Life Ministries in Bath, NY where we served for 21 years. In addition to speaking, I edited their newspaper; hosted a radio call-in show for several years, and taught missionaries how to raise support.

Milt: You and Jane moved to Bath, New York in how was this different from Wisconsin?

Jack: The Wisconsin ministry was small; just three of us on staff. I had spoken for the New York ministry several times, and in the summer of 1987 the Executive Director asked me to pray about joining staff. At the time Family Life was a large youth ministry, with a very low frequency radio station. As time went on the radio network expanded to dozens of signals across New York and Pennsylvania. As I noted, we were in Bath, NY for 21 years. I served as the Staff Evangelist for Family Life, the editor for the newspaper, hosted a call-in program on the radio network.

I continued to speak at several camps each summer. In 1993 we met a 13-year-old girl at a Wisconsin camp. She stayed in touch with us constantly, until the fall of the year when she tearfully told us she was pregnant. One thing led to the other, we had a family meeting, prayed about it, and ended up adopting our daughter, Janelle, at birth, November 4, 1994. It was horrifically expensive as the birth mother was a minor, there were two states involved, and the red tape was astronomical.

Several years later I received a call, and a young woman told me her name and asked if I remembered her. I told her, "no, I don't." She explained she was part of our ministry teams a few years prior. I then remembered her, and remembered she had dropped off the planet suddenly. She asked if she could meet, and my wife and I made arrangements to meet her in a local restaurant.

When she walked in, I was pretty certain of what she wanted to speak, she was very pregnant. In our conversation she told us she ran away from home, got pregnant in New York City; had an abortion... got pregnant again and couldn't go through with another abortion. She remembered us and the story of Janelle...and asked us if we would consider adopting her baby.

On April 10, 2002 Jacob Richard Isaiah Hager was born into our family. Neither of the adopted children were in my five-year plan; but God has big sleeves, and sometimes has "tricks" up those sleeves.

The days continued to pass, and the radio network was rapidly increasing. As it did, I could see the writing on the wall that the youth ministry aspect was going to be left in the proverbial dust.

I was in contact with Mike Mosiman who was the Dean of Students at CUBI in Kansas City for a long time and moved to St. Joseph to take over the ministry here. We were also connected through the Bible Quiz Fellowship National tournaments, both serving on the leadership board.

One day in 2007 Mike and I were discussing some quizzing issues, and Mike perceived that I wasn't really happy at Family Life. Mike said: "Why don't you come to St. Joe and do whatever you want to do?" I thought that was a pretty good job description! Jane and I prayed over the possibilities and we resigned from Family Life and moved to Missouri in 2008 to serve with Midland Ministries. My title is 'Ministries Liaison', the same as it was in New York. There is a staff of 12, and I assist with staff development and encourage everyone to expand their knowledge base to better our audience. I continue to be involved in prison speaking, both locally and nationally with "Behind the Walls."

Milt: As a former prison inmate, you were drawn back to the prison system in Missouri. Do you recall your first visit back behind bars, although under new circumstances?

Jack: The first time preaching in a prison took place way back in 1980 at the age of thirty-three. I came in touch with Curt Shoop through an introduction from his wife working at Kansas City for Christ. He was operating the M2-Heart of America Jobs Therapy in regional prisons which was the way to bring Christian influence into the prison and connect the prisoners with potential employers upon their release. He asked me to come to Lansing Prison which is near Leavenworth. Even today when I enter a prison and the heavy doors clang behind me, I get shivers up my spine. There is no sound in the world like the iron gates slamming together. But once inside,

I don't want to leave. It's the relationship thing where the prisoners understand my message because I at one time walked in their shoes. I'm comfortable speaking in prison.

About that same time the Chuck Colson movie "Born Again" came out and in KC, Colson was at the premier showing. He asked if there were any x-cons in the audience and several of us stood up. He and I chatted after the movie, and he invited me to Leavenworth to speak with him. I was cleared into Leavenworth and after the event he asked me to be his Midwest Director for Fellowship. Twenty years later I met him in Buffalo, New York and re-introduced myself and asked if he remembered me. He said: "Back in those early years if you had a pulse and an x-con I wanted you on my staff".

[As a new Christian, Chuck Colson voluntarily pled guilty to obstruction of justice in 1974 and served seven months in Alabama's Maxwell Prison for his part in the Watergate scandal. In his best-selling memoir, Born Again, Chuck wrote, "I found myself increasingly drawn to the idea that God had put me in prison for a purpose and that I should do something for those I had left behind." Colson emerged from prison with a new mission: mobilizing the Christian church to minister to prisoners. In 1976, he founded Prison Fellowship, which is now the nation's largest Christian nonprofit serving prisoners, former prisoners, and their families, and a leading advocate for criminal justice reform. In recognition of his work among prisoners, Colson received the prestigious Templeton Prize for Progress in Religion in 1993. Chuck Colson passed away April 21, 2012. His legacy continues, however, in the work of Prison Fellowship and in the lives of the many people his ministry has touched. After a career in hardball politics, Chuck Colson emerged as one of the most influential evangelical leaders of the past half century, devoting his life to ministering to prisoners and sharing the Gospel's message of love and hope to millions.]

Milt: I am trying to imagine what the atmosphere is like inside the prisons when you counsel and pray with the inmates. Jack: Prisons are like churches…each one has a different feel, atmosphere, and procedures. A maximum-security prison is way different than a medium or minimum facility. At the same time, prison is prison…a place where men (and women at the "doll house," or women's facility) are forced to live in a constricted environment with some not-so-nice people. In many ways, at least to me, life in a max is worse than combat. At least in Vietnam we had some idea who the bad guy was, some clue as to what might happen. In prison every day, every hour, every moment has the potential for something totally unexpected to happen. You basically wake up each morning recognizing you could be dead before the day ended, and for no genuine reason.

When I go into prison I almost always go in as a preacher. The inmates who come to chapel are like the people who come to church on the street. Some are Christians, some are curious, some are there just hoping to see a skirt, or to just get out of the cell block.

People too often say to me, "Jack, why do you waste your time preaching in prison! Aren't there are lot of phonies who come to chapel?" And I tactfully reply, "Sure there are…why should prison church be any different than your church?"

Milt: You are unconventional in your style; so, were you ever challenged on your credentials?

Jack: Not to my face. I've never been asked directly about my 'sheep skin'. I operate under the word-of-mouth referral process. When one pastor makes a positive recommendation to another pastor, that's all that counts. I am not against higher education, but I'm more in favor of internships and the Bible study group approach where one does not incur huge debt the rest of their life simply to get a degree.

Milt: What is the 'Bible Quiz Fellowship'?

Jack: It is a program where teenagers are on teams of seven to compete against other teams. They memorize a chapter or up to five chapters of material. Each year we have different books of the New Testament; if a teen stays involved for seven years he or she will quiz over the entire New Testament. I love our style of quizzing as it is not random verses, but consecutive verses in consecutive chapters…thus teaching the teens the vital importance of context.

During the competition interrogative questions are asked, such as "According to John 3.16, Who so loved the world?" with the answer, of course, being "God." The competition can be intense, with competitive quizzers watching the quizmaster's mouth to see if he is forming a "who" or a "what" etc. As soon as they think they know the question/answer they leap to their feet triggering a light in front of the quizmaster, who stops immediately and then the recognize quizzer has 20 seconds to provide the correct question and the right answer without giving any extra info. It is hard to explain in words, but I've been involved as a quizmaster since 1978 and the teens continue to amaze me. Obviously, our hope is that the verses are not simply memorized, but lived out.

Milt: It has now been decades since January 30th, 1974 and your conversion. And now honoring me to collaborate with you to write your story, how do you describe these past, soon-to-be five decades? Jack: It has been a great adventure. When I got out of prison, if someone had told me that I was going to become a fulltime minister speaking all over the country and the world, and in all types of venues; I'd have call them nuts. But that is what happened. I think a lot of Christ-followers feel, perhaps subconsciously, that to be in God's will is to be miserable, or in some level of vocational ministry.

But to serve the Lord should not be a burden, but a joy. Is it easy? Of course not. Jesus said, "Marvel not that the world hates you." James wrote, "Consider it all joy when (not "if") you encounter various trials." Paul admonishes us to "exalt in our tribulation," and the Word declares "all those who desire to live godly in Christ Jesus will suffer persecution."

I frequently tell people that I am amazed I get to do what I get to do. God could use a donkey...there may be some similarities. Whether it is a one-on-one discussion or counseling session, meeting with a senior group, or at a youth camp, church conference, in prison, or a rally of 7,000, I self-reflect: "What am I doing here, and how did I get here." I am beyond grateful to have a bride..and a few friends... who are not afraid to put me in my place if I start to get a big head.

Milt: In 1973 you picked up a book of inspiration and the Bible to read in the Texas jail. Now, decades later maybe someone will pick up your book to inspire him or her in a positive direction and change. Jack: I pray so. This fits my personality to have an oral history instead of a book with fancy prose. Years ago, in jail I picked up a book that led me to the Bible, that led me to Christ. I would be blessed beyond measure if someone reads this book and finds some hope.

Maybe their life is a mess and the story can give them a hint that they can change. It may be another prisoner who thinks he is a victim of the system; but then with this book may help him take responsibility for his actions paving the way for real change.

My primary goal is that people find Christ as their Savior, and if this book helps in that process, that is my dream. I am not a traditionalist, and my book is not traditional. When I met you in your driveway, I told you that people for decades said: "Jack, you need to write a book."

That God-directed stop at your garage sale allowed me to meet you, for our initial conversation to take place, and then for your offer to write the book. For that I am grateful both to God and you. Thank you.

Milt: We have spent private time in this interview process that will become an oral history. It is not a novel, it is not a biography, but tells your story in your own words. I know that I must have missed something along the way. What else comes to mind to complete your story?

Jack: The importance of marrying Jane. Always be a learner, whether by listening or reading. Trust God. Do right until the stars fall... Bob Jones, Sr. used to say that. Strive to love God and love people. See every day as a challenge and not a threat. The root of the word enthusiasm is God within you. Be excited about this thing called life! Redeem the time. I have a mission statement that I've worked out over the years...it is rather simple, but guides my planning, preparing, and progress:

I desire to know Jesus intimately,
so I can love Jesus intensely,
and to serve Jesus intentionally,
while helping others do the same.

Near the end of this chapter, Jack said: "What am I doing here, and how did I get here." Jack Hager. I'd like to take a shot at Jack's rhetorical question.

- A scotoma (scotomas or scotomata) is an area of lost or depressed vision within the visual field. Mental scotoma is an area within the visual field in which perception is distorted or entirely lost. I've recognized for years that teachers, historians, journalists, politicians, and others suffer from scotomas (going blind) both mentally and visually when discussing certain topics where bias creeps into certain subject matters. People tend to see things through a distorted lens and their perception is filtered through preconceived notions, or thoughts.

Likewise, every person does have 'blind spots' or scotomas. Until being incarcerated, Jack was never exposed to the Bible until he picked it up in the San Angelo, Tom Green County Jail. Jack Hager recognized his blind spots for Jesus Christ when he both mentally and visually began to expose himself to the Bible. Being jailed, alone, isolated, and frustrated his scatoma was removed and he became enlightened with growth to expand his public arena. As a result of his life experiences, high intelligence, and uncanny ability to relate the depth and breadth of the Bible, Jack helps anyone and everyone to accept Jesus Christ and make meaningful change while they remove their own scatomas.

As we were finishing the draft for this book, I wrote to Chaplain Jack, and told him:

Jack, I submit that your book is NOT about you. You are NOT writing it with yourself in mind. You are NOT looking for credit,

NOT looking for praise. You only use your example, your story and life's experiences as a learning tool so the reader reflects, thinks, and takes action for good on their own.

The book really sets the tone and validation for "predominant thought(s)" because you understand that all thoughts become things. You understand that whatever a person thinks, she/he becomes. You understand that all people move in the direction of their 'predominant thought(s)'. If one thinks negative…she/he does negative things. If one thinks positive…he/she does positive things. All thoughts become things and one's future is based on what he/she thinks. Your book is about removing the blind spots people have and maximizing their potential for good work by first helping them change their thoughts…then actions follow.

Jack, your thoughts prior to being arrested were selfish, self-centered, me, me, me, self-serving…then you changed your thoughts through conversion of your thoughts to Jesus Christ and good work. Your book is about purposeful thinking about self, self-image, and more importantly about others, no matter who they are…moving in one direction to the Lord."

JACK: Milt, my corrective to your kind words is that it is all Jesus. Yes, I try and strive to submit to Him, I discipline myself to stay in the Word of God and prayer…but as my favorite song says, "In Christ Alone my hope is found,.."

Milt: Now that your story is completed, I have a follow up question. America is embroiled in the secular movement which is permeating all parts of our society. What is your impression of secularism and its impact on values, people, the church and society at large?

Jack: Well, we could write another entire book or two on that subject! The Bible says "But know this: Hard times will come in the last days. For people will be lovers of self, lovers of money, boastful, proud, demanding, disobedient to parents, ungrateful, unholy, unloving, irreconcilable, slanderers, without self-control, brutal, without love for what is good, traitors, reckless, conceited, loves of pleasure rather than lovers of God, holding to the form of godliness, but denying its power," (1 Timothy 3.1-5)

Does that indictment not ring true of today?

Genuine Christ-followers, as opposed to churchers, are a minority. These days are full of change, and our culture is so open-minded that anything goes. They are "tolerant" of just about anything…except for someone saying, "I know the truth; and I want you to know the truth."

People talk about "my truth," but there is no such thing…there is only truth. And Jesus said, "I am THE way, THE truth, and THE life, no one comes to the Father except through Me." (John 14.6)

You maybe can get away with saying Jesus works for you, or that Jesus is one of many ways to heaven (as Oprah Winfrey has written, "The biggest mistake humankind makes is to say there is only one way to whatever you perceive God to be.")

But once you declare Jesus is truth and that salvation through Him is the only way to forgiveness and reconciliation with God…you are "narrow-minded" and called a bigot, or worse. Yeah, I'm narrow minded on this topic. The Bible says, "wide is the road to destruction, but narrow is the path that leads to eternal life, and few there are that find it."

I pray...yes, I pray, that this book is used by God to help people find truth...and truth IS Jesus.

Milt: I've noticed on your Facebook postings that you apparently enjoy photography in communicating your experiences. When traveling to new towns, small villages and cities; you frequently visit the local cemeteries and appear to be reflecting on old tombstones. You also take frequent photographs of colorful sunsets and sunrises.

Jack: When I was a kid my dream was to be a photojournalist for National Geographic. I do enjoy taking pictures (and am very grateful I don't have to buy film...thank you, smart phone). All my life I've been fascinated by cemeteries and headstones; don't know why. I think it serves as a reminder as to the brevity of life...it all comes down to that dash, as in 1942-2008 or whatever. I want my life to count, regardless of the cost. I also am struck by the words on many stones, whether a Bible verse or some other saying. I wonder why those words were picked. I see the tragedy of early death, the evidence of a life well lived on some stones. As far as sunrises and sunsets...I admire the colors, the uniqueness...and I am thankful I can look at beautiful things and know Who to thank.

Why me Lord? What have I ever done, To deserve even one, Of the pleasures I've known?
Tell me, Lord, What did I ever do, That was worth lovin' you, For the kindness you've shown?
Lord help me, Jesus, I've wasted it so, Help me, Jesus, I know what I am
But now that I know, That I needed you so, Help me, Jesus, My soul's in your hands
Try me, Lord, If you think there's a way, I can try to repay, All I've taken from you

Maybe, Lord, I can show someone else, What I've been through myself, On my way back to you

Lord help me, Jesus, I've wasted it so, Help me, Jesus, I know what I am

But now that I know, That I've needed you so, Help me, Jesus, My soul's in your hands

Lord help me, Jesus, I've wasted it so, Help me, Jesus, I know what I am

But now that I know, That I've needed you so, Help me, Jesus, My soul's in your hands

Jesus, My soul's in your hands Songwriter: Kris Kristofferson, 1973©

Tragedy of Suicide

The draft copy of Jack Hager's oral history was within a few days of being edited and ready for print when a horrific tragedy occurred once again that ignited another significant emotional event (SEE) in the life of Jack and for his family, friends, associates and most of all for the family of a teenage suicide. I asked Jack if he wished to address suicide for inclusion in his book; without violating the privacy of the family concerned. MT

Jack: There are far too many cliches regarding suicide. "A permanent answer to a temporary problem." "The most selfish thing a person can do." Though both those sayings have truth in them, until someone has been in the shoes of potential suicide, we've no idea.

Even with my seasonal depression the last few years I have never thought of ending my life. I can't relate with wanting to check out. But like the 14-year-old girl who shot herself recently, I've not dealt with major issues. She had a weird recently diagnosed disease wherein certain sounds thundered in her head and made it extremely hard to concentrate, and apparently caused lots of pain.

Just before she ended her life she wrote, "I love you, Mom. I love you, Dad. I love you, Janet (her twin sister). I love Jesus, and I've asked Him to forgive me, but I just can't take it anymore."

I can't relate to that. I wish she could have talked to someone in those closing moments. They say this disease primarily strikes highly intelligent girls going through puberty. That describes my friend very well. I know of too many other suicides. In most cases I don't know the 'whys'.

I know it is under-reported, because well-meaning doctors cover it up. It is rampant among young people. Why?

I don't pretend to know...it's easy for people to blame culture, cellphones, or a host of other reasons. There is no one-size-fits-all answer; and Christians are not immune. The only advice I can give... if you are ever contemplating suicide...reach out to someone. If there is no one reach out to me!

And if you ever hear anyone even "joking" about committing suicide, get help immediately. Love them enough to risk them hating you.

ONE FINAL NOTE:

If you ever want to discuss anything written here; if you ever want to discuss the Christian faith; if you ever just need a listening ear... connect with me...

Jack Hager
Midland Ministries
709 E. Hyde Park Avenue
Saint Joseph Mo 64504
jack.hager@gmail.com 816 261 1881

I blog at www.youcanknowjack.com and have a podcast, "You Know Jack – the Podcast"

Addendum-

Below are eight quotes from thousands that I extracted from lengthy reviews/letters from attendees to Reverend Hager's presentations for your review.

...Mr. Hager got a standing ovation from our student body for his straight forward presentation......I recommend Mr. Hager to any secondary school principal who has the good fortune to have the opportunity for such an assembly. Dr. M.D. McKenney, Dodge City High School.

...I can safely say that you're address was the most thought provoking and appropriately targeted to the student body of any that we have experienced at North. Thank you for your sensitivity to the special problems that we have in high school with the separation of church and state. Paul D. Longhofer, Principal, Wichita High School North.

...In my twelve years at Wyandotte High School, I have never experienced any presentation that so motivated and inspired our assembly. Your story is one of courage and I salute you. Keep up the good work and 'fight the good fight'. You are most definitely being guided by God. Robert D. Tichenor, Student Council Advisor, Great Plains Teens for Christ. Phillipsburg, KS

…It was, without a doubt, the best all-school assembly we have had in my five years at Gardner Edgerton High School. Mr. Hager's manner of presentation is excellent and his subject matter is even better. His talk concerned crime, drug abuse, alcohol and tobacco. One could hear a pin drop in the auditorium for the entire presentation. Tom Trigg, Principal, Gardner Edgerton High School

…Your topic encouraged young people to assume responsibility for their own behavior, and has been echoed throughout our students' junior and high school careers. We appreciate your generosity to spend the entire day with Haverling staff and students. Sandra C. Zaidel, Guidance Council and Administrator, Haverling Central High School

…The program was absolutely outstanding, down to earth, non-offensive to minority or morality groups. There was no vulgarity used and no religious indoctrination in the presentation other than stating that God was the reason for the change in Mr. Hager's life. Wm. D. Hughes, Principal-Chillicothe High School

…Jack is blunt and doesn't beat around the bush which relates to the youth. They learned that Christ is the only answer for living today and into the future. My daughter now has developed a vital personal daily devotional as a result. Thomas Mathews, Camp Director-Crescent Lake Bible Camp Rhinelander, Wi.

…Youth and adults alike seek Mr. Hager's counsel and advice because he is very direct, frank, and honest. He has been the vital staff member of Family Life Ministries for the past sixteen years and has made presentations to civic clubs, inmates at local and federal prisons, churches, high school assemblies, and adult group with excellence. Dick Snavely, FLM Founder-Bath, NY

9 781489 740571